UNIQUE
.... ## OREGON

A GUIDE TO THE STATE'S
QUIRKS, CHARISMA, AND CHARACTER
....

RICHARD HARRIS

John Muir Publications
Santa Fe, New Mexico

John Muir Publications, P.O. Box 613, Santa Fe, New Mexico 87504

First edition. First printing June 1996.

Library of Congress Cataloging-in-Publication Data
Harris, Richard, 1947–
Unique Oregon : a guide to the state's quirks, charisma, and
character / Richard Harris. — 1st ed.
   p.   cm.
   Includes index.
   ISBN   1-56261-247-6
1. Oregon-Guidebooks. I. Title.
F874.3.H37 1996
917.9504'43—dc20   95-52136

Editors: Rob Crisell, Peggy Schaefer, Elizabeth Wolf
Production: Janine Lehmann, Nikki Rooker
Graphics Manager: Sarah Horowitz
Design: Nobul Graphics
Typesetting: Marilyn Hager
Illustrations: Art Parts™/Fonthaus Inc.
Maps: Deborah Reade
Photo Research: Deborah Brink
Printer: Publishers Press

Distributed to the book trade by
Publishers Group West
Emeryville, California

Front cover photo: Leo de Wys Inc./William P. Kraus
Back cover photo: Leo de Wys Inc./Marie Ueda

CONTENTS

WELCOME
···············to OREGON

It's hard to imagine a more scenic state than Oregon. The Pacific Ocean licks sand-dune beaches and crashes on rocky headlands as glacier-covered volcano cones tower 11,000 feet above sea level. Ancient coastal forests loom so thick overhead that no ray of sunshine reaches the ground. Even the rain becomes a fine mist as it filters through the leafy canopy, while on the other side of the mountains, surrealistic stretches of barren sand-and-rock landscapes come alive with brilliant hues of red, yellow, and turquoise.

Visitors to Oregon are struck by the contrast between the "wet side" of the state on the ocean-facing slope of the Cascade Range and the completely opposite character of the east-facing "dry side." It's more than a simple matter of topography or climate. The local people go out of their way to make sure visitors understand that they are not like the odd characters who live over on the other side of the mountains, where the typical resident does/doesn't play tennis in the rain, drives/doesn't drive a pickup with a gun rack, eats/doesn't eat mollusks raw, is/isn't accustomed to driving two hours to the nearest convenience store for a microwave burrito.

But Oregonians also have certain

character traits in common. They value the uncrowded space and go to great lengths to discourage population and development from spilling out of neighboring California and across the state line. They take pride in their rich history and can tell you exactly where Lewis and Clark came through the place that would become their town. They live close to nature and find meaning in a glimpse of a bald eagle, a gray whale, or a herd of pronghorn antelopes. They glory in their affinity with Oregon natives who became celebrities—folks like musician Doc Severinsen, actress Lindsay Wagner, Nobel Prize winner Linus Pauling, cartoonist Matt Groening, and President Herbert Hoover.

Despite the depredations of a timber industry whose practices have been a subject of controversy for decades, ecotourism comes easy in Oregon. Whether it's a stroll through a peat bog in search of carnivorous plants, a trek into high mountain wilderness in the company of a llama, or a birdwatching expedition to a lake improbably located in a desert, new discoveries await the casual visitor and lifelong resident alike.

Unique Oregon is a compilation of one-of-a-kind destinations, historical insights, and fun facts. It is designed for curious and adventuresome travelers of all ages. Open to any page and you will find readable, entertaining information. The index guides you to specific topics and sites. The table of contents is organized so that you can tell at a glance what subjects are covered in each section. However you choose to use this book, you'll soon discover what's so unique about Oregon.

Oregon's Roosevelt elk

D.D. Pepin/Oregon Tourism Division

OREGON

Population: 2,842,321
Area: 98,386 sq. miles
Capital: Salem
Nickname: Beaver State
Date of Statehood:
February 14, 1859
Highest Elevation: Mount Hood
11,235 ft.
State Flower: Oregon grape
State Bird: Western meadowlark
State Tree: Douglas fir
State Motto: The Union

THEN
and NOW

PREHISTORIC OREGON

Twenty-five million years ago, a huge fissure suddenly split the shallow seabed and filled eastern Oregon with molten basalt 500 feet deep—one of the world's largest lava flows, covering an area of 225,000 square miles.

The oldest evidence of humans living in Oregon is a sandal discovered in a cave at Fort Rock State Park, which has been carbon-dated to about 11,000 B.C.

200 million years ago: Oregon lay at the floor of a tropical sea off the west coast of a supercontinent that was slowly splitting apart to become Europe, Africa, and North and South America. As it drifted westward, the North American continental plate scraped over the hard rock floor of the Pacific Ocean, which ground soft underwater parts of the continental shelf into rocky rubble.

100 million years ago: The westward-drifting North American continental plate pressed the rock floor of the eastern Pacific Ocean deep enough into the earth that the rock began to melt. The molten rock burst to the surface to form volcanic islands, which grew in size as they continued to spew ash and lava for the next 65 million years.

35 million years ago: The weight of North America finally fractured the Pacific Ocean floor, causing huge volcanic eruptions 100 miles offshore which continued for 10 million years. The volcanoes—which would become the Cascade Range—formed a solid land mass, isolating submerged Oregon from the Pacific as an inland sea. Molten rock and ash gradually filled the sea.

Steve Terrill/Oregon Tourism Division

WHERE TO SEE PREHISTORIC WILDLIFE

John Day Fossil Beds

● ●

In the beginning, eastern Oregon was subtropical forest inhabited by a variety of prehistoric mammals. Twenty-five million years later, in the 1860s, a cavalry troop crossing the desolate **John Day Desert** found a pile of fossilized bones.

Today, three of the main fossil areas are now units of **John Day Fossil Beds National Monument**. The Island in Time Trail in Blue Basin takes visitors to the spots where fossilized turtles, saber-toothed cats, oreodonts, and miniature horses were found. The original fossils are now in museums, but cast reproductions have been half-buried in their places. In the Painted Hills Unit, the Leaf Fossil Hills Trail reveals the fossil record of an ancient rainforest. *FYI: Monument Headquarters, HCR 82, Box 126, Kimberly, OR 97848; 541-987-2333.*

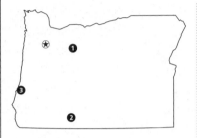

OREGON'S INDIANS

• •

The **Nez Percé**, or **Saahaptin**, people were the most powerful tribe in northeastern Oregon when the first non-Indian settlers arrived. They were moved onto a reservation in Oregon's Wallowa Valley in 1855, but when gold was discovered in the region, they were forced to relocate to a new reservation in Idaho. Some members of the tribe refused to move, touching off the famous Nez Percé War in 1877.

Their leader, Chief Joseph, led 450 refugees on a trek across the Bitterroot Mountains and into Montana attempting to reach Canada, but they were captured a few miles before reaching the border. The surviving Nez Percé refugees were sent to Oklahoma, but later transferred to a reservation in Washington. The descendents of the people who did not go with Chief Joseph still live on the Idaho reservation today.

The **Modoc** people in the mountains of southwestern Oregon fought the whites in the Modoc War (1863–64). The Modoc leaders were hanged by the army at Fort Klamath 7 miles south of Crater Lake National Park. Oregon's Fort Klamath is now in ruins except for a restored guard house containing exhibits about the Modoc War.

A closely related tribe, the **Klamath** people—who maintained peaceful relations with settlers diring the war—now share a reservation with the Modoc.

INDIAN RESERVATIONS IN OREGON

• •

The largest Indian reservation in Oregon is the **Warm Springs Reservation** (1) in the north central part of the state. Descendants from a number of Paiute and Shahaptian groups who inhabited the inland mountain areas of Oregon, including the Des Chutes, John Day, Tenino, and Tilkuni tribes, share the reservation with the Wasco people, one of several Chinook tribes that lived along the Columbia River.

Thirty-two years after the federal government ceased recognizing the tribe, the **Klamath Indian Reservation** (2) regained federal recognition again in 1986. The tribe hosts the Chief Schonchin Days Powwow, including a parade, Indian rodeo, and arts and crafts show, in Klamath Falls on Memorial Day weekend each year.

All coastal tribes in Oregon were "terminated" by the federal government in 1956 as part of a policy "to assimilate the Indians into the dominant society." The Indians responded by petitioning for recognition as the **Confederated Tribes of Coos, Lower Umpqua and Siuslaw** (3). In 1984, they gained federal recognition— and a 6.1-acre reservation at Coos Bay. The Siletz people regained federal recognition in 1977. In 1980, 3,800 acres were returned to the tribe.

The Umatilla, Walla Walla, and Cayuse people, tribes closely related to the Nez Percé, share the **Umatilla Reservation** in eastern Oregon.

Olney Patt, Jr.

The Museum at Warm Springs

MUSEUM AT WARM SPRINGS

Artifacts from past centuries are exhibited to the public, as well as replicas of a traditional lodge and a song chamber. An art gallery shows works by Indian artists of the Pacific Northwest.
FYI: 2189 Highway 26, Warm Springs, OR 97761; 541-553-3331.

EXPLORATIONS BY SEA

• •

1543—Spanish sea captain Juan Rodriguez Cabrillo sails northward to map the Pacific coast. The first European to see the shore of Oregon, he does not land there. A small-boat expedition led by Cabrillo's pilot, Bartolome Ferrelo, approaches the mouth of the Columbia River but cannot land because of the strong current.

1544—Cabrillo dies, leaving Ferrelo in command. The crew sails back to New Spain (colonial Mexico), discovering San Francisco Bay along the way. Since they did not set foot on the Oregon coast, they cannot legitimately claim it for Spain.

1579—British privateer Francis Drake sails up the Pacific coast as far as Oregon. Naming the territory New Albion, he claims it in the name of Queen Elizabeth I. It is a hollow claim, however, because no other British ship will reach Oregon for another two centuries.

1603—Spanish navigators Aguilar and Vizcaino claim Oregon in the name of the King of Spain. Their claim, however, is as groundless as Drake's.

1741—Russian explorer Vitus Dane claims the territory on behalf of the Czar. Russian fur trappers begin making their way down the coast from Alaska to the Pacific Northwest, but fail to establish a permanent settlement in Oregon.

1763—France cedes the Louisiana Territory to Spain in the treaty ending the Seven Years' War. Even though its only major colonial port is 2,000 miles away, the territory includes Oregon.

1778—Following his discovery of the Sandwich Islands, British sea captain

From 1604 to 1740, Indians of more than two dozen tribes lived on the Oregon coast, oblivious to the fact that their land had been claimed by both Spain and Britain.

Corbis-Bettmann

James Cook reaches the Oregon coast on his third round-the-world voyage, planning to return to England via the rumored Northwest Passage, which did not exist. In his search, he named practically every bay and point along the Oregon coast after one saint or another.

1791—During his second voyage around the world, Boston sea captain Robert Gray sails the Oregon coast and claims the land on behalf of the newly formed United States of America.

1792—Commissioned to map the Pacific coast of North America, British sea captain George Vancouver renews Queen Victoria's claim to the territory. Now four nations—Spain, Russia, Britain, and the United States—claim Oregon as their own, even though none of them has built a single settlement there.

Queen Elizabeth knighting Sir Francis Drake in 1581

The Astoria Column tells the story of Oregon's early pioneers

EXPLORATIONS BY LAND

1800—In a secret treaty, Spain returns the Louisiana Territory to France on condition that it would not be transferred to any other colonial power. The 828,000-square-mile territory extends from the Mississippi River to the Pacific Northwest coast. France makes no serious attempt to establish a settlement west of the Mississippi.

1803—Desperate for funds to finance Napoleon's conquests in Europe, France sells the Louisiana Territory to the United States for $15 million, most of which President Thomas Jefferson borrows from British banks. The acquisition more than doubles the area of the United States—in theory, at least.

1804—President Thomas Jefferson names his personal secretary, 29-year-old Captain Merriweather Lewis, to lead an exploration across the Louisiana Territory to the Pacific Coast. Congress authorizes a budget of $2,500 for the expedition, which will include 35 men—one-twentieth of the entire U.S. Army at that time. Lewis selects Lieutenant William Clark, 33, an old friend and skilled mapmaker as his travel partner.

1805—After a 4,000-mile trip from the trading outpost of St. Louis across what will become the states of Missouri, Iowa, Nebraska, South and North Dakota, Montana, Idaho, and eastern Washington, the Lewis and Clark expedition reaches the Columbia River near the site of present-day Umatilla, Oregon, in October.

1807—Although Spain and Russia relinquish their claims to Oregon soon after news arrives of Lewis and Clark's accomplishment, the British Hudson's Bay Company commissions fur trader David Thompson to set up forts and trading posts throughout the Northwest to keep American trading companies out of the region. Thompson focuses his efforts on the area north of the Columbia River, so the first American traders move into the territory south of the river.

1811—American fur trader John Jacob Astor establishes Fort Astoria, directly across the Columbia River from the Hudson's Bay Company's Fort Vancouver. Astoria will grow into the first permanent non-Indian settlement in Oregon.

1818—The United States and Great Britain enter into an agreement for joint occupation of the Oregon Territory (which includes Washington and part of Idaho), putting an end to years of hostility and occasional violence between the two major trading companies.

Of their sojourn on the Oregon coast in 1806, Clark writes: "Winds violent, trees falling in every derection, whorl winds, with gusts of Hail & Thunder— Oh how disagreeable our Situation dureing this dreadful winter."

Pioneers on the Oregon Trail in a 1993 reenactment

SIGHTSEEING WITH LEWIS AND CLARK

Historical markers commemorating the Lewis and Clark expedition in Oregon are located at The Dalles, Seaside (where the pair built a salt cairn to mark the end of their journey) and Ecola State Park near Cannon Beach. More extensive interpretive exhibits about the expedition can be found at **Fort Clatsop National Memorial** (*FYI: U.S. 101, Astoria; 503-861-2471*), **Bradford Island Visitors Center** (*FYI: Bonneville Dam; 541-374-8820*), and the **Oregon High Desert Museum** (*FYI: U.S. 97, Bend; 541-382-4754*).

PIONEERS

●●●●●●●●●●●●●●●●●●●●●●●●

1829—Inspired by Lewis and Clark's published journals, Boston teacher Hall Kelley forms the American Society for Encouraging the Settlement of the Oregon Territory and distributes pamphlets extolling the wealth and beauty of the region, which he has never seen.

1832—Unable to raise government funding, Kelley mounts a small, underequipped expedition bound for the Oregon Territory by way of Mexico. In New Orleans, Kelley's followers rob him and leave him stranded. Kelley continues alone and, wracked with malaria, finally reaches California. There he joins a hunting party and, with them, finally makes it to Oregon. Unfortunately, the party is riding stolen horses. Kelley is arrested, jailed at Fort Vancouver, and eventually deported to Hawaii.

1834—Rev. Jason Lee establishes his mission in the Wilamette Valley. The mission itself will become Willamette University.

1842—Physician Elija White, upon being appointed federal Indian agent for the Oregon Territory, organizes the first wagon train bound for the Willamette Valley. The 120 pioneers follow the route mapped earlier in the same year by Lieutenant John Fremont and his guide, mountain man Kit Carson, which will come to be known as the Oregon Trail. Before the completion of the first transcontinental railroad 27 years later, 350,000 pioneers will follow the Oregon Trail—more than all other westward routes combined.

END OF THE TRAIL

• •

The **End of the Oregon Trail Interpretive Center**, which opened on Abernathy Green in Oregon City in June 1995, is housed in three buildings built in the shape of giant covered wagons. One of the buildings is a multimedia theater where the story of the Oregon Trail pioneers is told with multiple projectors and special effects. Other exhibits include a replica of a Missouri provisioner's store (the beginning of the trail) and the actual end of the trail, where the first pioneer community in Oregon was established. *FYI: 1726 Washington Street, Oregon City, OR 97045; 503-557-1151.*

Another museum commemorating the Oregon Trail is near the town of Baker, almost 300 miles to the east of Oregon City. **The National Historic Oregon Trail Interpretive Center** stands atop Flagstaff Hill, where pioneers got their first glimpse of the Cascade Mountains in the far distance. The center overlooks a section of the original trail marked by wagon ruts, still visible after 150 years. There are also four miles of hiking trails. *FYI: Located 5 miles east of Baker on Highway 86; 541-523-1843.*

U.S.D.I. Bureau of Land Management

Entrance to the National Historic Oregon Trail Interpretive Center

The Oregon History Center

Upon hearing that gold has been discovered in northern California in 1848, almost all Oregon residents abandoned their homesteads to move south. The territorial legislature had to cancel its session because so many elected representatives had left the state.

STATEHOOD AND SETTLEMENT

● ●

1845—Portland is founded under the name of "Stumptown."

1846—Great Britain gives up its claim to joint occupancy of the Oregon Territory.

1847—Henry Lewelling brings the first 700 fruit trees to Oregon, planting them in his Willamette Valley orchards. The apple, cherry, pear, and plum saplings have been hauled by wagon all the way from Iowa.

1849—Henry Lewelling transports his first crop of 100 apples to San Francisco to sell. Fresh fruit is scarce in the California mining camps, where scurvy (caused by a lack of vitamin C) is a leading cause of death. Lewelling's apples sell for the phenomenal price of $5 each—about the cost of room and board for a week. Newcomers pouring into California create lucrative markets for many Oregon products, from lumber to eggs, and new settlers soon swell the population of the Willamette Valley to record levels.

1853—Washington Territory splits off from Oregon Territory, leaving the Oregon boundaries that exist today.

1854—Oregon voters reject statehood because they cannot agree on whether to enter the nation as a free state or a slave state. A movement begins to declare Oregon an independent republic. Statehood initiatives are also voted down in 1855 and 1856.

1857—Oregon becomes a state on Valentine's Day. Oregon City, the largest town in the territory, is the capital.

1860—The Portland-based Oregon Steam Navigation Company gains a monopoly on shipping up and down the Columbia River. In the next decade, the city's population will grow by 1,200 percent.

1862—The state capital moves to Salem.

1870—Portland becomes the largest city in the Pacific Northwest—a ranking it will hold until 1897, when the Alaska gold rush will bring boom times for Portland's arch rival, Seattle.

1883—The first railroad arrives in Portland, enabling agricultural and forest products to be sent to market in eastern cities and triggering the most rapid economic and population growth rates in Oregon's history. Beef, salmon, and timber become huge industries.

OREGON HISTORY CENTER

The story of human life in Oregon from the first nomadic Indians to the Portland Trail Blazers pro basketball team is the focus of the Oregon History Center in downtown Portland. The center contains five stories of artifacts, dioramas, and multimedia exhibits.

FYI: 1200 W.W. Park Avenue, Portland, OR 97205; 503-222-1741.

The Ku Klux Klan, which once had a membership of more than 25,000 in Oregon, elected Klan leader Walter Pierce as governor in 1922, sponsored legislation that barred Catholic schools in the state, and attempted to rescind Oregon's ratification of amendments to the U.S. Constitution guaranteeing blacks citizenship and the right to vote.

TWENTIETH-CENTURY OREGON

1907—Congress repeals the Forest Preservation Act of 1891, opening up millions of acres of forest in Oregon and four other northwestern states to commercial timber cutting. Ten days later, President Theodore Roosevelt, a conservationist, responds by setting aside vast forest reserves in Oregon and other states and prohibiting all timber operations there. The reserves will eventually become the national forest system under a compromise arrangement that allows limited timber leasing.

1908—Oregon becomes the first state to limit working hours for women to 10 hours a day, as the U.S. Supreme Court in the landmark case of *Muller v. State of Oregon* upholds the constitutionality of the maximum hours law.

1915—World War I brings a burst of economic growth in the shipbuilding and timber industries. Of the thousands of workers who come to Portland's shipyards, the majority are African Americans.

1919—Oregon becomes the first state to put a tax on gasoline.

1937—Bonneville Dam, the first hydroelectric dam on the Columbia River, begins operation. It is the creation of U.S. Engineer Henry Kaiser, who also designed Hoover Dam in 1931 and Grand Coulee Dam in 1941.

1938—When the salmon run unexpectedly drops off, the first fish ladder is built at Bonneville Dam to let salmon swim upriver to their spawning grounds. Because of the salmon shortage, fishermen

Oregon Tourism Division

Portland skyline at sunset

venture farther off the Oregon coast and discover large schools of albacore tuna. The Columbia River Packers Association opens a tuna cannery next to its salmon cannery in Astoria and trademarks its brand name, Bumble Bee.

1953—Oregon growers harvest their first million-barrel cranberry crop as demand for cranberry products reaches an all-time high.

1959—The federal Food and Drug Administration orders all cranberries from Oregon off the market after discovering that a tiny portion of the crop is contaminated by residue from a hazardous chemical weed-killer. Media coverage causes a panic, and sales of cranberry sauce drop nearly to zero. The National Cranberry Association responds to the bad press by changing its name to Ocean Spray and introducing several new cranberry products, including cranberry juice cocktail.

The Oregon legislature ratified the 15th Amendment to the U.S. Constitution in 1959, guaranteeing blacks the right to vote 89 years late.

THE NATURAL WORLD

Mount Hood and Hood River County

OREGON'S VOLCANOES

The Cascade Mountains of the Pacific Northwest boast more volcanoes than any other American mountain range north of Central Mexico. From Mount Hood on Portland's misty eastern horizon to Mount Mazama in the southern part of the state, volcanoes stand as towering landmarks throughout the Cascades.

After the cataclysmic 1980 eruption of Mount St. Helens blanketed Portland in gray ash, the U.S. Geological Survey analyzed the major dormant volcanoes in the Cascades. They named Mount Hood among those most likely to erupt next— with a 50-50 chance that a large eruption will occur in the next 5,000 years.

Today Mount Hood, Oregon's highest mountain at 11,235 feet, is one of the state's most popular year-round resort zones, offering three downhill ski areas in winter and hiking, horseback-riding, and llama trekking in summer.

Another Oregon volcano, **Mt. Bachelor**, erupted 12 to 14 million years ago out of an 8-mile-long crack in the ground. Lava from this eruption stopped up rivers and created basins which eventually became the emerald-blue lakes for which Oregon is well known. You can see many of these lakes scattered alongside the Cascade Lakes Highway (Highway 46).

Bob Jensen

Obsidian flow at Newberry National Volcanic Monument

SIGHTSEEING IN THE LAVA FIELDS

• •

For a panoramic view of Oregon's volcanic landscape, drive up the spiral roadway to the top of **Lava Butte**, a small volcanic cone south of Bend. The great volcanoes you can see from an observation deck on the highest point of the crater rim include Mount Bachelor, Oregon's largest ski resort area, and the Three Sisters. Near the base of the Lava Butte, Lava Land visitors center serves as a starting point for volcanic sightseeing highlights at **Newberry National Volcanic Monument**. Other unique natural features of the volcano field include **Lava Cast Forest**—the remains of giant trees engulfed by 20-foot-deep volcanic flows—and the mile-long Lava River Cave, the longest lava tube in Oregon.

FAREWELL, MOUNT MAZAMA

The last major volcanic outburst was Mount Mazama in 4860 B.C. The 12,000-foot-high volcano exploded with a force 40 times that of Mount St. Helens, throwing rock and ash across 5,000 square miles. The resulting crater was six miles across. When it filled with water to a depth of 2,000 feet, it created Crater Lake—the deepest lake in the United States.

Big Bend River near Breitenbush Hot Springs

For a close-up look at the high-altitude lava flows north of the Three Sisters, take Highway 242 over Old McKenzie Pass, west of Bend. As you reach the 6,324-foot summit, you cross vast lava flows within six miles of the towering Three Sisters Peaks.

GETTING IN HOT WATER

• •

A reas where volcanoes have erupted in the past often have geothermal hot springs, and Oregon is no exception. There are 16 known hot springs in Oregon. Here are a few of them:

1) Kah-Nee-Ta Resort: The Confederated Indian Tribes of Warm Springs regained ownership of the hot springs for which their reservation was named in 1957 as compensation for loss of their traditional fishing grounds, flooded by The Dalles Dam. The Indians built the plush Kah-Nee-Ta Resort. Guests at the hot springs can opt to stay in authentic tepees or more conventional rooms. The Warm Springs tribes still fish elsewhere on the Columbia River, relying on the traditional method of stabbing the salmon from the riverbank with sharpened poles, to serve at Kah-Nee-Ta's weekly Native American–style feasts. *FYI: 541-553-1112 800-831-0100.*

Breitenbush Hot Springs: Near the town of Detroit in the central Cascade springs have become a New Age resort complete with yoga classes, vegetarian meals, and even firewalking lessons. Besides flowing into the spa's hot tubs and natural bathing pools, the hot springs warm the rustic guest cabins. *FYI: 503-854-3314.*

3) Cougar Reservoir: If you prefer an all-natural hot-springs experience, check out the ones at Cougar Reservoir on the McKenzie River, 50 miles east of Eugene. Popular with the area's sizeable hippie population, the springs have been dammed with rocks to form soaking pools. To reach them, turn right at the reservoir dam and go 3½ miles to the marked trailhead.

4) McCredie Hot Springs: Southeast of Eugene near the town of Oakridge are McCredie Hot Springs, near Highway 58 on Salt Creek, and Kitson Hot Springs near Hills Creek Reservoir.

5) Old Perpetual: Oregon's only continuously spouting geyser, Old Perpetual sits outside the town of Lakeview, luring birdwatchers and the occasional sightseer who wanders into the remote reaches of southeastern Oregon.

6) Hot Springs Campground: Northeast of Lakeview, Hart Mountain National Antelope Refuge's Hot Springs Campground features a 104-degree soaking pool in a concrete privacy enclosure.

7) Alvord Hot Springs: Even deeper in the Oregon outback is Alvord Hot Springs. Located in the Alvord Desert 22 miles north of the tiny ranching community of Fields, the springs feed a concrete soaking pool. There is no charge to use them.

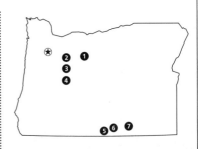

OREGON CAVES NATIONAL MONUMENT

There's really only one cave at Oregon Caves National Monument, but it's the largest one in the state. The labyrinth winds for more than a mile through a mountain of white marble, taking visitors through room after room dripping with stalactites, flowstone curtains, and natural columns.
FYI: 541-592-3400; south of Grants Pass.

Steve Terrill/Oregon Tourism Division

Oregon Caves National Monument

UNDERGROUND OREGON

• •

The type of cave most typical of Oregon is the lava tube, formed during volcanic eruptions as hot gas vents its way to the surface of a molten lava flow. The most often-visited of these is Lava River Cave in **Newberry National Volcanic Monument** near Bend. It is the longest known uncollapsed lava tube in the state. Visitors can take an hour-long self-guided tour of the cave. Bring your own flashlight or lantern, or—in summer only—rent one at the cave entrance.

Oregon's southeastern desert is also a spelunker's playground. **Malheur Cave**, on Highway 78 east of Malheur Lake, for instance, is a huge subterranean lava bubble—a high, wide-domed chamber without side passages. Inside the cave is a chilly 30-foot-deep lake. In the same vicinity, but only accessible by four-wheel-drive or horseback, is the **Saddle Butte Lava Tube Area**, an 80-square-mile lava field honeycombed with caves.

OREGON'S GRAND CANYONS

• •

Carved by the second-largest river in North America, the **Columbia Gorge** west of Portland slices the Cascade Range in half, separating Oregon and Washington. The Columbia Gorge Scenic Highway takes sightseers close to the steep cliffs that drop as much as 3,200 feet from the mountain wilderness above the rim. Streams plunge over the edge to form spectacular waterfalls.

Michael Clapp/Oregon Tourism Division

With a drop from the rim to the river averaging more than 6,500 feet, **Hell's Canyon** is the deepest gorge in North America. Carved by the Snake River on the boundary between Oregon and Idaho, it is the central feature of Hell's Canyon National Recreation Area in Oregon's northeast corner. Motorists can reach Hell's Canyon Overlook easily or—for an even more dramatic view—drive on unpaved roads to Hat Point Overlook at the highest point on the rim. Most of the 70-mile-long canyon must be reached by hiking, horseback riding, llama trekking, or by taking a whitewater raft expedition or jet boat tour. *FYI: Hell's Canyon National Recreation Area, Highway 82, Enterprise, OR 97828.*

Lunch break on a trip through Hell's Canyon on Snake River

The Columbia Gorge is so wide that motorists on nearby Interstate 84 (on the Oregon side) may hardly notice they are in a canyon at all.

Oregon Dunes National Recreation Area

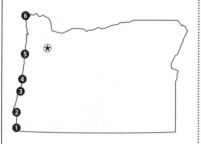

UNIQUE BEACHES

Given their frigid temperatures, Oregon beaches are better for beachcombing, romantic walks, and sunbathing than for swimming. The good news is, Oregon's 200 miles of public beachfront are uncrowded and beautiful. Here are some of the most distinctive beaches:

1) Harris Beach State Park and **Samuel H. Boardman State Park** north of Brookings are known for their abundance of driftwood. The most beautiful spots include Whalehead Beach—where an offshore rock seems to spout like a whale as waves strike it—and Indian Sands. The parks also include several natural bridges and arches extending above the sea from coastal cliffs.

2) Cape Blanco State Park, near the town of Sixes, has one of the few stretches of black sand beach in Oregon, as well as a picturesque lighthouse.

3) Sunset Bay State Park near Winchester may well be Oregon's most idyllic beach. It is set on a small, round, secluded bay so picturesque and romantic that the Douglas fir trees lining the beach almost seem as if they ought to be coconut palms.

4) Oregon Dunes National Recreation Area, near the town of Florence, is certainly the most spectacular beach on the Oregon coast. Some of the cream-colored sand dunes are more than 500 feet high— taller than those of the Sahara Desert. Formed over thousands of years as waves have eroded coastal sandstone formations and cast the sand up on the beach, the sand dunes extend 45 miles up and down the coast. The dune field is up to two miles wide, so reaching most beach areas means hiking across it. Hiking trails, which start at several campgrounds along U.S. 101, are invisible across the open sand. Hikers follow wooden posts to find the way. *FYI: Oregon Dunes NRA, 855 Highway Avenue, Reedsport, OR 97467; 541-271-3611.*

5) Agate Beach near Newport is a favorite of beachcombing rockhounds. Among the small stones strewn along the broad, hard-packed beach are semiprecious or collectible ones such as jasper, tiger eye, and moonstone. The Newport Chamber of Commerce hands out a pamphlet telling people how to hunt for them.

6) Beach Drive is the only place in Oregon where motorists are allowed to drive their cars on the beach. It is located between Gearhart and Fort Stevens State Park.

Cape Lookout State Park

Shelley Metcalf/Oregon Tourism Division

Ocean temperatures in Oregon are chilly enough to cause hypothermia in as little as 20 minutes.

View of the lake at Portland's Crystal Springs Rhododendron Gardens

GARDENS GALORE

May is the time to see rhododendron bushes in colorful bloom in Portland's **Crystal Springs Rhododendron Gardens** (*FYI: 503-256-2483*) and Eugene's **Hendricks Park Rhododendron Garden** (*FYI: 541-687-5324*), where the array of flowering shrubs also includes wild roses, forsythia, and dahlias.

FANTASTIC FLORA

The cobra lily attracts insects with its sweet-smelling nectar—and then eats them. When a fly or bee enters the plant's flowerlike mouth, stiff hairs keep it from going back out, but allow it to go farther down into the hollow stem, where the tempting pool of nectar turns out to be the plant's digestive system. One of the best places to find this macabre little green carnivore is **Darlingtonia Botanical Wayside**, a sphagnum moss bog with a paved half-mile nature trail. The free, state-owned wayside 4 miles north of Florence is named for the lily, known to botanists as *Darlingtonia californica*.

Wild azaleas bloom in May along the southern Oregon coast. Five varieties of these scarlet or orange flowers can be seen in **Azalea State Park**, off Highway 101 at Brookings. Daffodils bloom in profusion in March and snow lilies in July in 10-mile-long **Samuel H. Boardman State Park** north of town, colorful proof that the Brookings climate is ideal for a multitude of flowering plants. Commercial growing of Easter lilies is a major industry in Brookings.

No springtime tour of Oregon in bloom would be complete without a drive along the farm roads of the Willamette Valley, a major commercial tulip-growing area. April displays the flowers in bloom in long, straight rows of pink.

While macrophyllum, the kind of rhododendron commonly found in Oregon, has evergreen foliage, a second native species called albiflorum has white blooms and deciduous leaves.

OREGON'S FAVORITE TREES

Oregon's state tree, the spirelike ever-green Douglas fir, is extremely common in all the mountain areas—and becoming more so all the time. When timber companies clearcut an expanse of forest, they invariably replant it with Douglas fir seedlings because they grow quickly and yield a relatively soft, light wood that is easy to saw and sand. Also, the Japanese—the largest consumers of Oregon wood during the 1980s—prefer Douglas fir for the nearly white color of the wood. Besides its use in the construction of houses and furniture, Douglas fir is the preferred material for making disposable chopsticks.

Much less common is the myrtlewood, a broadleafed, tall evergreen tree that grows no place else on earth except southern Oregon's Coast Range. Its wood is far too precious to slice into lumber. Instead, each tree that is cut becomes material for artisans.

FYI: Oregon Myrtlewood Factory, Route 101 south of Bandon, 503-347-2500; House of Myrtlewood, 1125 S. 1st Street, Coos Bay, 541-267-7804.

The Douglas fir is named for Scottish botanist David Douglas, who first identified the species while exploring Oregon in 1823. Douglas fir is the preferred material for making disposable chopsticks.

Common murres at Gull Island

OREGON FOR THE BIRDS

• •

The **Klamath Basin**, which contains three national wildlife refuges in the southern Cascades extending down to the California state line, is the world's largest wintering area for bald eagles. Many of the majestic birds roost in the tall trees of the ancient forest on the southern outskirts of the town of Klamath Falls. In the spring and summer, thousands of white pelicans inhabit the area. The center of attention for birds and birdwatchers is **Klamath Lake**, where more than a million ducks and geese congregate during spring and fall migrations.

Crane Prairie Reservoir, on the Cascade Lakes Highway southwest of Bend, has a large population of American ospreys (also called fishhawks). Once a vanishing species, these eaglelike raptors are now common at the reservoir. If you visit between April and October, you may see one diving from hundreds of feet in the air to grab a fish in its razor-sharp talons.

The several bird sanctuaries along the Pacific coast include **Cape Meares**, **Three Arch Rocks**, **Gull Island**, and **Oregon Island**. Perhaps the best place on the coast for a close-up view of seabirds and wading birds is **South Slough Estuary** near Coos Bay. The estuary "breathes," becoming freshwater at low tide and saltwater at high tide and nurturing shellfish for bitterns, egrets, and great blue herons to dine on.

The marbled murrelet is a small, rare seabird that nests only in remnants of ancient coastal rainforest around Cape Perpetua and the town of Yachats. It became a subject of controversy when local environmentalists, seeking to create a forest reserve, sued to stop logging by alleging that the forest was off-limits under the Endangered Species Act as a critical habitat for the bird. The suit was dismissed in 1995, and today birders can hope to spot the marbled murrelet only in the **Commins Creek Wilderness** near Cape Perpetua or the **Rock Creek Wilderness** near Hecata Head.

MALHEUR NATIONAL WILDLIFE REFUGE

Established by President Theodore Roosevelt in 1908, **Malheur National Wildlife Refuge** encompasses several shallow lakes, including the large Malheur Lake and Harney Lake, in a basin surrounded by a vast expanse of desert. The oasis of the lakes near Burns in eastern Oregon attracts nearly 250 native and migrating bird species, including trumpeter swans, pheasants, and Canadian geese.

WHALEWATCHING MADE EASY

● ●

The Oregon coast is one of the best places on earth to watch whales. In December, as huge gray whales migrate southward on their 6,000-mile journey to breeding and calving areas in Pacific bays of Baja California, their route brings them close to the Oregon coast. At the peak of the southward migration, around Christmas, the whales swim past at an average rate of one every two minutes at a speed of about four knots per hour. The return trip to summer feeding grounds in the Bering Sea between Alaska and Russia peaks in late March, though mother whales with new calves swim more slowly, and some may not reach the Oregon coast until early May. The whales travel farther from shore on the northward trip.

Binoculars are better than telescopes for spotting whales. When trying to spot a whale, watch for a cloud of spray above the water. One of these spouts is made when a whale exhales air through its blowhole. The whales usually travel in small "pods" or families.

FAVORITE WHALEWATCHING SPOTS

One factor making the Oregon coast especially good for whale-watching are the high headlands that afford sweeping views of the ocean. Whales typically swim closer to the shore at these points. Some popular places to whale-watch from land are **Umpqua Lighthouse**, **Cape Perpetua**, **Depoe Bay**, and **Cape Meares**.

Roy Lowe, USFWS

MORE MAMMALS AT SEA

• •

Stellers sea lions at Rogue Reef

Sea lion rookeries can be seen at many locations up and down the Oregon coast. The best known is the commercially operated **Sea Lion Caves** 11 miles north of Florence (*FYI: 541-547-3111*), the only sea lion colony on the mainland. Viewing the sleek creatures requires binoculars at most other sea lion viewing areas, such as **Seal Rock State Park** near Waldport. The sea lions, which can weigh more than a ton, are protected under the Endangered Species Act, making them about as popular with coastal fishermen as spotted owls are with loggers. Fishermen attribute any decline in catches to the predatory pinnipeds.

*Another endangered species on the rebound along the Oregon coast is the sea otter. Once on the verge of extinction, otters can now be seen frolicking around rocky offshore islands at such places as **Battle Rock State Park** and **Cape Blanco State Park** in the vicinity of Port Orford.*

LEAVE IT TO BEAVERS

· ·

The official reason the state of Oregon adopted the beaver as its mascot is that the animal's industrious nature reflects the character of human Oregonians. It is (officially) mere coincidence that the earliest non-Indian residents put the Oregon Territory on the map by hunting these giant rodents for their fur—which was used to make hats—and their musk glands, used in making perfume.

The beaver was on the verge of extinction by the time Oregon became a state in 1859. Thanks to legal protection, the beaver has made a strong comeback and is now found in many parts of Oregon. Modern forestry experts have learned that—far from being a nuisance as previously thought—the beaver plays a key role in Oregon's forests. The ponds that the beavers create with their dams quickly become habitat for a wide range of fish and amphibian species that other species depend on for food. The ponds also provide excellent sources of drinking water for many forest species. Over a period of 100 years or more, the ponds fill with silt to become fertile meadows essential to the health of the forests.

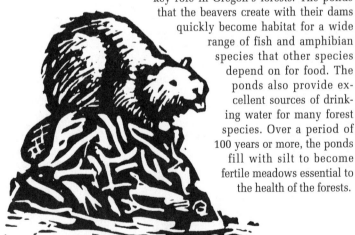

Larry Geddis/Oregon Tourism Division

SAVING THE SALMON

• •

Salmon-fishing on the Willamette River

The Columbia River has the largest salmon runs in the world. Born in mountain streams, the fish migrate to the ocean where they spend their adulthood. Then after a period of years—apparently following a sense of smell so sharp that it defies imagination—the fish make their way back upriver to precisely the same stream where they were born to spawn and die.

During salmon runs, thousands of on-lookers gather to witness the spectacle of fish scrambling their way over the dams. Between 700,000 and 1 million adult fish climb the ladders every year as they make their way home to mate and die, and from 30 million to 50 million young fish travel down the fish ladders each year on their journey to the ocean.

*When **Bonneville Dam** was built in 1937, salmon fishermen were horrified to see the salmon begin to die out when their homeward route was blocked. As a result, fish ladders—pools arranged like flights of stairs to allow the fish to climb up and over the dams— were built alongside this and all other dams on the river.*

GOING to TOWN

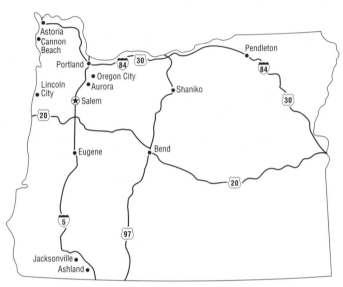

SALEM

Population: 116,950
Elevation: 171 feet
Noted for: State Capitol, Mission Mill Village, Bush's Pasture Park, Court-Chemeketa Historic District, Willamette University
Nearby: Silver Falls State Park, Willamette Mission State Park
Visitor's Information: 503-581-4325 or 800-874-7012

SALEM EVENTS

July—Salem Art Fair
August—West Salem Waterfront Festival, Oregon State Fair

SALEM

Two of the oldest buildings in Oregon are the house and parsonage of Rev. Jason Lee, who founded a Methodist mission on the Willamette River in 1834. His mission grew into the community of Salem. In 1842, the missionaries started Willamette University, the first college in the west. Salem existed in the shadow of Oregon City until 1852, when the capital was moved to Salem.

Jason Lee's homestead and parsonage are still standing and can be seen in Mission Mill Village, an open-air historical museum that is Salem's sightseeing highlight after the State Capitol itself. The gold-leafed statue atop the capitol's towerlike dome represents the pioneer spirit that brought early settlers to Oregon, and relief sculptures of Lewis and Clark and a covered wagon flank the capitol steps. Inside, an observation area in the dome offers a magnificent view of Salem and the Willamette Valley.

PORTLAND

● ●

Portland, the largest city in Oregon, is one of America's most beautiful cities. Its setting—on the banks of the Willamette River with Mount Hood and Mount St. Helens on the horizon—and the many public and private rose gardens throughout the city are among the factors that help make Portland so attractive. Equally important is an environmentally aware city government. Even in 1905, a Portland mayor proposed demolishing the buildings on alternate blocks throughout the city and replacing them with shady parks and rose gardens. Although the idea never came to fruition, the sentiment is echoed in Portland's Park Blocks, a grassy 25-block-long promenade with fountains on the west side of downtown, and Tom McCall Waterfront Park, also 25 blocks long, on the east side along the river.

Portland is the third-largest U.S. shipping port on the West coast. Major exports include forest products and wheat. It is also a major center for electronics manufacturing.

The "Artquake" festival in Portland

Mount Burns/Oregon Tourism Division

PORTLAND

Population: 495,482
Elevation: 77 feet
Noted for: International Rose Test Gardens, Portland Art Museum, Oregon History Center, Oregon Museum of Science and Industry, Tom McCall Waterfront Park, Yamhill and Skidmore/Old Town Historic Districts, American Advertising Museum, Trail Blazers pro basketball, Washington Park Zoo, Portland State University
Nearby: Columbia Gorge Scenic Highway, Bonneville Dam, Mount Hood, Ridgefield National Wildlife Refuge
Visitor's Information:
503-222-2223 or 800-962-3700

PORTLAND EVENTS

June—Rose Festival
July—Waterfront Blues Festival
September—Artquake
December—Parade of Christmas Ships

Hendricks Park

EUGENE

Population: 120,572

Elevation: 422 feet

Noted for: University of Oregon, Spencer Butte Park, Hendricks Park Rhododendron Garden, Owens Memorial Rose Garden, Howard Beauford Recreation Area, Willamette Science and Technology Center, Oregon Aviation & Space Museum

Nearby: Armitage State Park, Hendricks Bridge, Elijah Bristow State Park, Lookout Point Lake, Black Canyon

Visitor's Information: 541-484-5307 or 800-547-5445

EUGENE EVENTS

June—Oregon Bach Festival
July—Oregon Country Faire
September—Eugene Celebration

EUGENE

● ●

The character of Oregon's second-largest city is shaped by two often-opposing presences: the 17,000-student University of Oregon and the factories that process huge quantities of logs from the surrounding forest into lumber and paper.

Eugene offers a lot in the way of outdoor recreation activities, from golf to whitewater rafting. Hiking trails abound, including the spectacular South Hills Ridgeline Trail in Spencer Butte Park. The citywide network of cycling and jogging paths is one of the finest in the United States.

Eugene also rates high marks for culture. The Hult Center for the Performing Arts provides the venue for the Eugene Symphony, Eugene Opera, Eugene Ballet, Oregon Mozart Players, and Oregon Bach

Festival. Modern sculpture dots the university campus alongside century-old, ivy-covered brick buildings.

The city is also noteworthy for its abundance of arts-and-crafts galleries. The largest concentration of shops selling leather, stained glass, ceramics, jewelry, handblown glass, and the like is the Firth Street Public Market. Artisans also show their wares at the lively downtown Saturday Market.

ASTORIA

The first permanent non-Indian settlement west of the Mississippi River, Astoria was founded in 1811 by John Jacob Astor's fur trapping and trading company near the place where the Columbia River flows into the Pacific Ocean. Astoria grew into a city of elegant Victorian buildings that rivaled San Francisco in size and splendor.

Astoria's importance as a shipping port declined with the growth of Portland, whose upriver location provided more shelter from Pacific storms. Today, history is Astoria's stock in trade and tourism its main industry. Travelers on scenic coastal Highway 101 stop over to admire the view from the Astoria Column, a 125-foot-high tower atop a 635-foot-high hill, visit Astoria's several historical museums, and stroll along streets lined with stately Queen Anne-style residences. The downtown area is filled with galleries, antique shops, and small cafés with river views.

Nearby are Fort Clatsop, a replica of the log fort built by Lewis and Clark, and Fort Stevens, the only U.S. military installation on the West Coast to be shelled by the Japanese during World War II.

ASTORIA

Population: 10,050

Elevation: 16 feet

Noted for: Columbia River Maritime Museum, Astoria Column, Fort Astoria, Heritage Center Museum, Captain Flavel House

Nearby: Fort Clatsop National Memorial, Fort Stevens State Park, Del Rey Beach

Visitor's Information: 503-325-6311 or 800-535-3637

ASTORIA EVENTS

April—Great Crab Feed and Seafood Festival

June—Scandinavian Midsummer Festival

The Captain Flavel House overlooks the Columbia River

Dennis Thompson/Unicorn Stock Photos

LINCOLN CITY

• •

L incoln City may not be the largest
town on the Oregon coast (Coos Bay
holds that distinction), but it's certainly
the busiest. Formerly five separate towns,
collectively known as the "Twenty Mira-
cle Miles," it became a single "city" in
1965. Its unparalleled growth rate is
largely due to the fact that it is at the end
of the most direct route from Portland to
the Pacific.

Located near the city center is *Lincoln
on the Prairie*, a 14-foot bronze sculpture
depicting Abraham Lincoln as a young
lawyer on horseback reading a book.
(Maybe it's a guidebook—he's a long way
from home.) Honest Abe's actual connec-
tion with Oregon is tenuous at best. In
1848, he was appointed to serve as the
first territorial governor of Oregon, but
his wife objected, so Lincoln turned
down the appointment and never set foot
in Oregon.

Cascade Head is a popular vantage
point for whalewatching, and Lincoln
City's broad beaches are so extensive that
they seldom seem crowded even on
weekends, when hordes of Portlanders
arrive. The traffic-clogged streets are another matter.

LINCOLN CITY

Population: 6,335

Elevation: 114 feet

Noted for: Devil's Lake State Park,
Drift Creek Covered Bridge, Canyon
Drive Park, Cascade Head

Nearby: Siletz Bay, Gleneden
Beach, Fogarty Creek State Park,
Neskowin Beach, Van Duzer Forest
Corridor

Visitor's Information:
541-994-2164 or 800-452-2151

LINCOLN CITY EVENTS

May—Spring Kite Festival
October—Fall Kite Festival

ASHLAND

• •

Ashland has more bed and breakfast inns per capita than any other town in Oregon, including Portland. The attraction that brings most visitors to this graceful little creekside community at the base of 7,533-foot Ashland Peak is, of course, the Oregon Shakespeare Festival—the oldest such festival in North America.

Shakespeare came to Ashland in 1935 thanks to an odd coincidence: an abandoned Chautauqua building was condemned and slated for demolition. Elizabethan buff Angus Bowmer noticed that, with its original roof removed, the structure's architecture was almost identical to London's Fortune Theater (c. 1600), where many of Shakespeare's plays premiered. Ashlanders re-furbished the building into a replica of the original open-air Shakespearean theater, and the rest, as they say, is history.

Especially during summer, tickets and lodging reservations can be hard to get, and the art galleries, antique shops, boutiques, bookstores, and cafés that occupy Ashland's Tudor-style buildings bustle with activity. The town empties out in late October, and in winter you can find the most elegant of B&B accommodations at manageable rates. Why go to Ashland in winter? Nearby Mount Ashland offers the finest skiing in southern Oregon, with 23 ski runs and 100 miles of cross-country trails.

Oregon Tourism Division

Actors at the Oregon Shakespeare Festival in Ashland

ASHLAND

Population: 17,725

Elevation: 1868

Noted for: Oregon Shakespeare Festival, Lithia Park, Southern Oregon State College, whitewater rafting

Nearby: Lake of the Woods, Mountain Lakes Wilderness, Tub Springs, Howard Prairie Reservoir

Visitor's Information: 541-482-3486 or 800-482-2350

ASHLAND EVENTS

Mid-February through October— Ashland Shakespeare Festival
December—Home for the Holidays Festival
February—Ashland Winter Festival

BEND

• •

The largest Oregon "dry side" town, Bend is the ideal base camp for outdoor activities on the eastern slope of the Cascades. Though the town got its start as a logging camp and ranching center, today Bend's economy turns almost entirely on recreation.

The towering ponderosa pine trees of Deschutes National Forest come right up to the edge of town, offering a year-round array of adventures such as hiking, mountain biking, whitewater rafting, fishing, canoeing, snowmobiling, and dogsledding. A 20-minute drive takes travelers to the Mount Bachelor Ski Area in the heart of the high Cascades, and further explorations reach the spectacular scenery of the Cascade Lakes and the Three Sisters volcanic peaks.

To the south lies a cluster of scenic areas that includes volcanic cones, lava caves, lava fields, and a unique lava cast forest. Formerly a national forest scenic area called Lava Lands, the volcano field was recently transferred to National Park Service jurisdiction to become Newberry National Volcanic Monument.

PENDLETON

••••••••••••••••••••••••••

The largest town in largely empty eastern Oregon, Pendleton is a cowboys-and-Indians kind of place where the Old West remains very much alive. Pendleton is best-known for its woolen mills, which produce premium-quality shirts, coats, and blankets sold throughout the world. The mills date back to 1893 and have been modernized with computerized robotic sewing machines, freeing human workers to focus on quality control. Visitors can take the popular free tour (*FYI: 503-654-0444*).

Less-known but equally fascinating, the Pendleton Underground Tour takes visitors through tunnels dug by Chinese residents in the 1880s to avoid racial persecution on the streets of town. The network of tunnels connects many historic buildings of the era, including the old Chinese living quarters, laundry, meat market, gambling den, bordello, and jail.

Pendleton has an abundance of lodging, which only fills to capacity during the famous Pendleton Round-Up rodeo. The rest of the time, the town makes an ideal base from which to explore the neighboring Umatilla Indian Reservation with its art institute, traditional dance company, and gaming facility. You can also explore the wilderness trails of the Blue Mountains and the hidden beauty of this undiscovered corner of Oregon.

Matt Johnson

A performer at the Pendleton Round-Up

PENDLETON

Population: 15,715

Elevation: 1,068 feet

Noted for: Pendleton Woolen Mills, Pendleton Round-Up, Round-Up Hall of Fame, Pendleton Underground Tours

Nearby: Umatilla Indian Reservation, McKay Creek National Wildlife Refuge, Emigrant Springs State Park, Umatilla Wilderness

Visitor's Information: 541-276-7411 or 800-547-8911

PENDLETON EVENTS

April and October—Pendleton Underground Comes Alive
September—Pendleton Round-Up and Happy Canyon Pageant

Sunset over Coos Bay

SEASIDE TOWNS

Highway 101 along the Oregon coast presents a parade of fascinating small towns. Here are a few favorites, in order from south to north:

Brookings: This small town is a major commercial flower-growing center. Azalea State Park, in town, is a riot of wildflowers in spring. Harris Beach State Park and Samuel H. Boardman State Park are known as great places for beachcombing. The town's main annual event is the Driftwood Show in April. ***FYI:*** *Visitor's information; 541-469-3181 or 800-535-9496.*

Gold Beach: Located at the mouth of the Rogue River, Gold Beach is Oregon's only federally designated Wild and Scenic River. Several companies operate half-day and all-day jet boat tours up the river through virgin forests and rugged canyons teeming with wildlife. *FYI: Visitor's information; 541-247-7526 or 800-525-2334.*

Coos Bay: The largest and most industrialized town on the Oregon coast, Coos Bay is dominated by the huge Mill Casino, which once had the capacity to produce 20 billion board-feet of lumber a year. Nearby are three spectacular coastal parks—Sunset Bay, Cape Arago, and Shore Acres—as well as Golden and Silver Falls State Park, which contains one of Oregon's finest stands of myrtlewood trees in addition to the waterfalls. Coos Bay hosts the Oregon Coast Music Festival in July and the Blackberry Arts Festival in August. *FYI: Visitor's information; 541-269-0215 or 800-824-8486.*

Florence: This town is often considered the premier resort town on the Oregon coast. Its location—midway up the coast adjacent to Oregon Dunes National Recreation Area, Jessie M. Honeyman State Park, Darlingtonia Botanical Wayside, Heceta Head, and the commercial Sea Lion Caves—makes it an irresistible vacation destination. It has all the best of the Oregon Coast in a tourist-friendly package. The major annual event is the Rhododendron Festival in May. *FYI: Visitor's information; 541-997-3128.*

Seaside: This rustic town was built on the spot where Lewis and Clark ended their westward explorations. Seaside was also the first coastal resort town in Oregon, founded in the 1870s. Seaside Aquarium at the end of the 2-mile-long beachfront promenade has emerged as the town's top tourist attraction. Seaside's biggest annual event is the World Cup Kite Competition in October. *FYI: Visitor's information; 800-444-6740.*

TOWNS
FROM THE PAST

OREGON CITY

This town of 15,000 people located on a bluff at the conjunction of the Willamette and Clackamass Rivers, 20 minutes south of Portland, was the first spot chosen by early settlers. Split in half by steep rock cliffs, the town operates one of only three municipally owned elevators in the United States to carry pedestrians from river level to the historic district atop the bluff. Among the town's visitor attractions are seven museums and the largest public observatory in the Pacific Northwest.

AURORA

With a population of 600, little Aurora is virtually the same size now as it was in 1856, when founder William Keil and his German-Dutch followers established a utopian religious commune. Today, Aurora is known for its antique shops. The **Old Aurora Colony Museum** (2nd and Liberty Streets; 503-678-5754) consists of five historic buildings from the 1860s filled with handmade furniture, antique quilts, tools, and musical instruments.

SHANIKO

Though it has only 30 present-day residents, Shaniko's sizeable population of Old Western ghosts is kept alive in memory by tourist trade boosters who have scavenged old buildings from other abandoned towns in the area to bolster Shaniko's image as Oregon's best-preserved ghost town. Shaniko's church is actually a schoolhouse brought from another location, and its "Boot Hill" cemetery is fictitious—the original town had neither a church nor a cemetery. Its history, however, is real. Shaniko boomed in 1900, when the arrival of a railroad spur line transformed it into "The Wool Shipping Capital of the World." But the town's glory faded ten years later when another railroad by-passed it. Many of Shaniko's buildings contain memorabilia from the boom era, and carriages and buckboards are parked around town. You can still rent a room in the historic old hotel.

JACKSONVILLE

Originally a gold rush town that boomed in 1851 and then went bust in 1852, Jacksonville never turned into a ghost town. Instead, it became one of Oregon's finest small-town historic districts. Visitors to the town discover storefronts and picture-perfect old-fashioned churches dating back to the 1850s. Each comes with its own story, such as the whitewashed wooden Methodist church, said to have been built with gambling winnings.

The local museum features a reconstruction of the photo studio of famous resident **Peter Britt**, a Swiss photographer who traveled throughout Oregon in the 1850s. His classic photos include the first images of Crater Lake. Another visual artist whose works are still prominently displayed, Norman Campbell specialized in realistic "windows" painted on blank walls. Much of today's population—about 2,000 people—are retirees in search of a more idyllic yesterday.

Old storefront in downtown Jacksonville

Stuart Wasserman/Oregon Tourism Division

Eugene Skinner's hometown

Brenda Matthiesen/Unicorn Stock Photos

WHAT'S IN A NAME?

While filling out the paperwork to incorporate the small riverbank settlement of Stumptown, founders Amos Lovejoy and Francis Pettygrove wisely decided that a name change would enhance the new town's chances for growth. The two flipped a coin to decide whether to rename it Boston after Lovejoy's home town or Portland after Pettygrove's boyhood home in Maine. Pettygrove won the toss. To this day, there is no Boston, Oregon, though near Coos Bay there is a little town called Bunker Hill.

Eugene, now the second-biggest city in Oregon, is named after founding father Eugene Skinner. Many towns carry their founders' last names, but few are called by first names, and originally Skinner, Oregon, was no exception. The name change to Eugene helped overcome the fact that settlers in the area referred to the settlement as Skinner's Mudhole.

On the east side of the mountains, where most towns have stayed small, there seems to have been a shortage of people respectable enough to name towns after. Both the towns of John Day and Dayville, appropriately set along the banks of the John Day River near John Day National Monument in the region of Oregon referred to as John Day Country, were named after—surprise!—John Day, a hunter who came to Oregon with a fur trading expedition in 1811. The story says that he got separated from his party, was robbed of his horse, gear, and clothing by a passing war party, and was left to wander naked in the desert.

Raving mad, Day was sent home to his family in St. Louis, so residents named the river after him, and practically everyplace else in the region.

Charlie Borland/Oregon Tourism Division

Sand castle building at Cannon Beach

CANNON BEACH

• •

Cannon Beach (pop. 1,330) was named for a cannon that washed up on the beach from an 1846 shipwreck. Today it is one of Oregon's leading artists colonies. Art galleries and gourmet food shops seem to be the town's economic mainstays. The centerpiece of the town's scenic appeal is Haystack Rock, just offshore.

Nearby Ecola State Park is an outstanding wildlife viewing area with seabird rookeries, a sea lion colony, and a resident deer herd. Cannon Beach events include the world's foremost sand castle contest in May, the Stormy Weather Festival in September, and the Dickens Festival in December. *FYI: 503-436-2623.*

TASTE
of OREGON

THE CRANBERRY ROUND-UP

The speed with which cranberries must be wet-harvested makes for a lively, colorful spectacle. Write the **Cranberry Growers Alliance** (PO Box 1737, Bandon 97411) for more information on where to watch the harvest.

BOUNCING CRANBERRIES

Cranberries are grown in bogs along the Oregon coast. The bitter red berries grow on vines with 4-foot-long stems and runners that fan out in all directions, making a challenging tangle when harvest time comes in October and early November.

Some cranberries are harvested by the old-fashioned "dry" method, picking them from the vines and selling them fresh to be boiled down into homemade cranberry sauce or dried and added to muffins or other baked goods. Today, however, the most widely used method is "wet" harvesting, which is more efficient for large-scale production. The bogs are flooded, and the cranberries float to the surface after being loosened from the vines with a special machine called a "beater." When the water's surface is covered with the small red berries, workers round them up.

At the processing plant, cranberries must be handled quickly. Wet-harvested berries will spoil unless they are frozen within a few hours. Sorting is done using a device that bounces them up and down. Giant fans blow the bouncing berries into big containers for freezing. They are then used to make cranberry juice cocktails or canned cranberry sauce.

Oregon Department of Agriculture

HOPPING THROUGH OREGON

• •

Oregon's famed hops

Twelve different varieties of hops—the bitter herb used to flavor beer—grow in the Willamette Valley, including the Cascade hop, often ranked as the world's finest hop. Farmers in the Klamath Basin also produce 30,000 tons of malt barley a year. In 1985, Oregon became one of the first states to pass a law allowing microbreweries to make their own beer and serve it in brewpubs right on the premises. Today, Portland boasts more craft breweries and brewpubs per capita than anywhere else in the United States. The **Oregon Brewer's Festival**, held in Portland's Tom McCall Riverfront Park each July, is the largest gathering of independent brewers in all of North America. *FYI: Oregon Brewers Guild, 510 N.W. Third Avenue, Portland, OR 97209; 503-295-1862.*

Oregon growers produce almost one-third of the world's supply of hops.

The Headlight Herald

Cows in Tillamook County

Each year, 180 million gallons of milk go into making 20,000 tons of Tillamook cheese.

WINE AND CHEESE

Tillamook County, Oregon's premier dairy farming region, has been producing fine cheese since 1894, when Canadian cheesemaker Peter McIntosh moved there. Since the valley's rich grasslands supported so many Holstein, Jersey, and Guernsey cows, cheesemaking provided something dairy farmers could export. Local farmers even built their own ships to carry cargoes of cheese.

Visitors can take a free self-guided tour of the giant cheese factory, operated by the Tillamook County Creamery Association, a collective owned by 196 member dairies. *FYI: 4175 Highway 101 North, Tillamook, OR 97141; 503-842-4481.*

OREGON WINERIES

Most of Oregon's 112 vineyards and wineries are located within the Willamette Valley, where the gentle climate and long growing season are ideally suited to growing grapes. Winemaking is a relatively new industry in Oregon; most vineyards now operating have been planted since the mid-1970s. An Oregon specialty is wine made from local raspberries, blackberries, and boysenberries.

An easy winery tour from Portland follows Highway 99 southwest through Newburg and Dundee, then Highway 221 south to Salem, where you can take Interstate 5 back to Portland. Oregon winetasting rooms located in the coastal resort towns of Seaside, Tillamook, and Lincoln City offer samples from all regions of the state.

Oregon Tourism Division

Laurel Ridge Winery in Forest Grove

POOR NO MORE

• •

Originally established in 1911, the old Multnomah County Poor Farm was bought in 1990 by brothers, Mike and Brian McMenamins, who transformed it into **McMenamins Edgefield**—a vineyard, winery, and brewery. McMenamins Edgefield has since grown to include lodging, restaurants, and conference and banquet space—all styled like a quaint European village near the west end of the scenic Columbia Gorge. Visitors can take a free tour of the winery, then stroll through beautifully landscaped gardens, admire the McMenamins art collection, and stay for dinner. *FYI: 2126 S.W. Halsey Street, Troutdale, OR 97060; 503-669-8610.*

The Oregon Wine Newspaper *is available at all wineries. It contains a schedule of wine events and festivals.* **FYI: 503-232-7607.**

A golden chanterelle mushroom

*A knowledgeable
mushroom hunter in Oregon
can earn $300 to $500 a week.*

FOREST FOOD

● ●

From Crater Lake to the Columbia River Gorge, the perpetually damp forests of Oregon's coastal mountains provide ideal growing conditions for some of the world's most sought-after varieties of gourmet mushrooms. Among the most prized are chanterelle, matusake morel, and oyster mushrooms.

Beginning in April and continuing through the first rains of autumn, motorists on two-lane secondary highways that wind their way through the national forests will often spot parked trucks with signs like "Buying Chanterelles—Top Prices Paid." The offers are directed to the thousands of people, both local residents and itinerant crop pickers who come to Oregon during mushroom season, to seek their fortune in the freelance fungus-hunting business. The pay is substantional, but is scant reward for the expertise needed to tell the difference between valuable mushroom species and inedible or even deadly poisonous varieties.

It doesn't take much formal training to try your hand at mushroom hunting. Study the chanterelles and morels for sale at farmers' markets or quality food stores—or even buy a couple to carry along for comparison. When you've collected mushrooms you think are edible, stop to ask a roadside buyer to identify them for you *before* eating any.

BERRIES AND MARASCHINO CHERRIES

• •

The bright red cherries that grace the tops of cocktails and ice cream sodas originated at Oregon State University in Corvallis, where researchers were looking for a way to preserve the fruit so it could be shipped to other states. Royal Anne cherries are first cured in a syrup containing a decoction from the maraschino plant, a native of Italy. They are then colored, pitted, and canned using a special process. Today, most maraschino cherries still come from the fruit orchards of Oregon's **Willamette Valley**.

In addition to its cherries, Oregon ranks number one in the United States in the production of berries. The state's farmers produce raspberries, blackberries, blueberries, strawberries, loganberries, and blueberries. Many of these varieties grow wild in the mountains as well as under cultivation. A favorite edible wild berry is the huckleberry, found on the slopes of Mount Hood and other peaks in the Cascade, Wallawa, Blue, and Klamath ranges. The best time to pick berries is between midsummer and midfall. Many orchards, especially during the fall, allow you to pick your own.

Among the many other crops sold at roadside fruit stands and farmers markets in the Willamette Valley during the summer are melons, honey, asparagus, rhubarb, corn, green beans, potatoes, and fresh organic herbs.

Seaside Chamber of Commerce

Razor clamming at a beach in Seaside

Favorite ways to eat Dungeness crabs are dipped in melted, seasoned butter or chopped up in a cocktail or salad.

HOW TO CATCH CRABS

● ●

Dungeness crabs, the favorite eating variety in Oregon waters, live on the sea bottom in most bays. The best time of year to go crabbing is in September through December, and the best time of day is during the least tidal current— around high slack tide or low slack tide. On days when the difference between high and low tides is small, the crabbing can be good all day.

Most people use motor boats for crabbing because more crabs are found in the outer part of the bay, but you can also catch them from fishing piers. To catch a crab, bait a crab ring (a wire basket on the end of a long rope or chain) with a small dead fish and lower it to the ocean floor. Leave it there long enough for a crab to discover it—but not more than 20 minutes, or the crab will have time to eat all the bait and depart. Then pull the crab ring straight up.

Cook crabs in boiling salt water, either live and whole or freshly killed and cut up, for about 15 minutes, then chill them in cool water to loosen the meat from the shell.

HOW TO CATCH CLAMS

Clamming is a popular family activity on Oregon beaches. All you need is a shovel or a potato fork. The time to go clamming is before low tide, when the water is retreating to expose wet sand flats. Clams bury themselves in the sand six inches to two feet deep and receive oxygen through small holes in the sand. Some clam species can be spotted by these holes, others by spurts of water when they breathe. When you locate one, all you have to do is dig down through the sand until you reach it. Dig fast. Some varieties can burrow into the sand very quickly to escape.

Keep clams alive in clean, cool water for several hours before cooking so they can expel the sand from their shells. Then pry the shells open with a knife, cut the meat away from the shell and cut off the black tip of the neck and all other dark-colored areas. Split the neck to remove the gills. After cleaning, the clams can be fried, cooked into a chowder, or steamed in their shells.

After cleaning, clams can be fried, cooked into a chowder, or steamed in their shells.

Jake's Famous Crawfish Restuarant

BAJA NORTE

Look for Oregon's best Mexican food at Baja Norte in Bend, featuring spicy south-of-the-border favorites with an occasional pinch of California flair.
FYI: 801 N.W. Wall Street; 541-358-0611.

EXCEPTIONAL EATERIES

• •

Fresh, locally grown ingredients and intriguing ambience characterize Oregon restaurants. Here are a few favorites:

Jake's Famous Crawfish has been a Portland favorite for more than a century. Besides the little crustaceans that gave this restaurant its name, Jake's has a lengthy seafood menu offering entrees that range from smoked salmon and raw oysters to clam chowder and bouillabaisse. *FYI: 401 S.W. 12th Avenue; 503-226-1419.*

Food from every corner of the globe is featured at Portland's **Harbor Side** restaurant. Here you'll find Chinese, Mediterranean, and Cajun specialties on a single menu—along with magnificent views of the harbor from booths on the upper level. *FYI: 1309 S.W. Montgomery Street; 503-222-6077.*

Perhaps the most elegant dining on the coast is at the **Sun Room in Salishan Lodge** near Gleneden Beach. Seafood—the staple cuisine in all coast towns—receives an extra "Oregon Nouveau" touch here, with tantalizing choices that range from shrimp salad sandwiches to steamed clams in thyme sauce. *FYI: Highway 101; 541-764-2371.*

The eclectic array of reasonably priced cuisines in Eugene's Fifth Street Market includes falafel, baba ganoush, and hummus in the Arabic-style **Casablanca** (*FYI: 541-342-3885*) and the exotic tastes of Thai curries at **Mekala's** (*FYI: 541-342-4872*) to old-fashioned malteds and cheeseburgers in an ambience straight out of the Fifties at **Terry's Diner** (*FYI: 541-683-8190*).

The spirit of the Old West lives on in Pendleton at the **Rainbow Bar and Grill**, an old-fashioned saloon, where beef is served in a dozen different ways amid photographs of past Pendleton Round-Up champions. *FYI: 209 S. Main Street; 541-276-4120.*

Coast travelers will find authentic Mexican food at the classic hole-in-the-wall **Rubio's** in Brookings, where the offerings include seafood tacos. *FYI: 1136 Chetco Avenue; 541-469-4919.*

America's largest soda fountain is just one of the attractions at the **Oregon Caves Chateau Restaurant** at Oregon Caves National Monument. The large restaurant offers old-fashioned ice cream sodas, burgers, and fries, along with thick steaks and a host of seafood selections. *FYI: 541-592-3400.*

Best-known among the numerous sophisticated dining establishments along Ashland's main street is the **Chatêaulin**, a classic French restaurant where entrees such as Oregon-grown free-range chicken in a wild mushroom sauce are served in a candlelight-and-stained-glass atmosphere. *FYI: 35 N. Main Street; 541-482-8818.*

Down the street, **Brother's Deli** offers an eclectic menu selection specializing in vegetarian and kosher items from lox and bagels to huevos rancheros. *FYI: 95 N. Main Street; 541-482-9671.*

RIMSKY-KORSAKOFEE

Portland's favorite bohemian-chic hangout, Rimsky-Korsakofee is hidden away in an old red house. People line up outside the door for dessert and latté, classical music, and stimulating conversation. *FYI: 707 S.E. 12th Avenue; 503-232-2640.*

BUILDING OREGON

CITY OF BRIDGES

Divided by the Willamette River and separated from neighboring Vancouver, Washington, by the Columbia River, Portland has more bridges than any other American city of comparable size. Named after the founder of the Oregon Hospital for the Insane, Steelbridge was originally known as the Asylum Street Bridge. Built two years later, Steel Bridge has two levels—one for cars and the other for trains—which can be raised and lowered independently. The city's only suspension bridge, the Gothic-towered St. John's Bridge, was the longest rope-strand suspension bridge in the world when it was completed in 1931. It was built by Joseph Strauss, the same architect who designed San Francisco's Golden Gate Bridge. Fremont Bridge, the city's newest and most expensive bridge (built in 1973 for $82 million), is America's longest tied-arch bridge. Its engineers earned a place in the Guinness Book of World Records by raising the bridge's 6,000-ton arch into place from the river with hydraulic jacks.

Although Oregon's covered bridges look like artifacts of an earlier century, most were actually built between 1936 and 1966.

Rick Schafer/Oregon Tourism Division

THE BRIDGES OF LINN COUNTY

• •

O regon has more covered wooden bridges—known in earlier times as "kissing bridges"—than any other state west of the Mississippi. Most of them are hidden away on narrow old highways used only by the locals. Many of Oregon's most picturesque bridges are in Linn County near Albany and Sweet Home.

For instance, motorists who take a 43-mile scenic detour from Interstate 5 by exiting at Albany, following U.S. 20 and S.R. 226 east, and then returning west on S.R. 22 to rejoin the interstate at Salem, will find marked back roads leading to Bohemian Hall Bridge, Hoffman Bridge, Larwood Bridge, Gilkey Bridge, Shimanek Bridge, Hannah Bridge, and Jordan Bridge.

Shimanek Bridge in Linn County

Shehar's Bridge *(c. 1850s) over the Deschutes River on Highway 216 is one of the few places in the state where you can still watch Indians practicing the traditional dip-net method of fishing from platforms during salmon runs.*

Klootchie Creek County Park near Seaside

SAVING THE LAST HABITAT OR TIMBER?

● ●

Oregon's most controversial bird, the northern spotted owl, lives only in ancient forests, making them a symbol for environmental activists to protect indirectly what present law does not protect directly. Although the small, elusive mouse-eating owls are impossible to count accurately because they only come out at night, they are classified as a threatened species under the U.S. Endangered Species Act because their habitat is in danger of vanishing. About 90 percent of Oregon's ancient forest has been cut down and replanted with fast-growing Douglas fir, leaving the owls homeless. In

1990, the federal district court issued an injunction making more than three million acres of ancient forest in Oregon off-limits to logging.

Loggers say their jobs, their families, and the forest communities in which they live are the ones endangered—thousands of jobs and millions of dollars are lost for the sake of a rarely seen bird subspecies. Environmentalists respond by saying that scaling timber harvests back to sustainable levels and protecting the remaining wilderness forests may cost jobs in the short run. In the long run, though, sound environmental policies will preserve some jobs in an industry that would otherwise self-destruct. Loggers, faced with widespread unemployment right now, find the argument unconvincing.

The northern spotted owl is not the only bird to bring Oregon logging to a screeching halt. In another 1990 case, the federal court issued a stay to block timber operations on thousands of acres of forest alleged to be critical habitat for a threatened bird called the marbled murrelet.

The court repealed the logging ban in 1995 due to lack of evidence that the birds could still be found in that part of the forest. Other endangered or threatened species that make their homes in Oregon's dwindling temperate rain forests include weasellike pine martens, pileated woodpeckers, and a species of vole known as *Phenacomys*.

Although federal law doesn't directly protect trees, the value of saving the ancient forest was revealed recently when scientists discovered that the Pacific yew—a shrub burned as trash when old forst was cut and cleared—contained the potent anti-cancer drug, aclitaxel.

If logging had continued at the same rate as in the 1980s, there would be no more ancient forest, and no trees big enough to be worth cutting down by the year 2000.

Weather machine in Pioneer Courthouse Square

PORTLAND'S OFFBEAT ARCHITECTURE

• •

Take a walking tour of downtown Portland and find out why it is known for its controversial public art and architecture. As you pass the **Georgia Pacific Building** in the 900 block of Fifth Avenue, for instance, you can't help but notice the white marble sculpture entitled *The Quest,* which local wags have nicknamed "Three Groins in the Fountain" (a project, they say, of the city's "Art in Public Places" program). Nearby, bounded by Sixth Avenue, Broadway, Morrison, and Yamhill streets, **Pioneer Courthouse Square** is a hodgepodge of unusual and mostly nonfunctional architectural elements that include wrought-iron fences and gates to nowhere, neoclassical columns (one of them intentionally collapsed with a chessboard on top), and a purple-tiled waterfall. Forty-eight thousand bricks bear the names of donors who helped make it all possible.

The ultimate offbeat building downtown (or, for that matter, anywhere in Oregon) is the **Portland Building** at 1120 W.W. Fifth Avenue. Designed by Michael Graves and billed as "the first major postmodern structure erected in the United States," it is pink, yellow, blue, and bizarre. On the Fifth Avenue side of the Portland Building is *Portlandia*, the largest hammered copper sculpture since the Statue of Liberty.

Balancing Portland's "postmodern" downtown architecture are two nearby historic areas—the **Yamhill** and **Skidmore/Old Town Historic Districts**. Both were built in the 1880s in a similar, lavishly Victorian architectural style.

Architecture in Portland's **Nob Hill** district resembles that in the San Francisco neighborhood for which it was named. Victorian townhouses and Georgian mansions, as well as more than 200 small shops and restaurants, make Nob Hill an enjoyable place to explore on foot.

BEACONS IN THE FOG

• •

The nine surviving lighthouses along the Oregon coast stand as monuments to the state's maritime past. Built by the now-defunct U.S. Lighthouse Board between 1870 and 1896 to warn ships away from rocky capes and headlands, the lighthouses were originally tended by resident lightkeepers who lived in small frame houses adjoining the brick beacon towers. In the 1960s, the U.S. Coast Guard installed automated beacons, the lighthouses were added to the National Register of Historic Places for preservation, and the lightkeepers had to move.

The only privately owned lighthouse in Oregon stands on **Tillamook Rock**, a 133-foot-high basalt islet more than a mile offshore between Cannon Beach and Seaside, accessible only by boat. The lighthouse, which is not open to the public, serves as a columbarium, a repository for the ashes of deceased people who have been cremated.

Don't miss the **Heceta Head Lighthouse** near the town of Florence. This beacon is thought to be one of the most-photographed lighthouses in the United States. It's also within eyesight of nearby **Sea Lion Caves**, about 10 miles north of Florence.

Oregon Tourism Division

Umpqua Lighthouse

LIGHTHOUSE TOURS

Of the nine lighthouses in Oregon, seven are open for tours. They are located off Highway 101 at **Cape Blanco**, **Coquille River**, **Umpqua River**, **Heceta Head**, **Yaquina Bay**, **Yaquina Head**, and **Cape Meares**. All are ideal spots for whalewatching and scouting storms.

Oregon Tourism Division

Portland's Pittock Mansion

AT HOME WITH HISTORY

● ●

A stately Portland residence-turned-museum, the **Pittock Mansion** (1) was built in 1914 by the publisher of Portland's daily newspaper, *The Oregonian*. The French Renaissance-style mansion has been restored using original family furnishings and artwork as well as antiques, many of them dating back to the 17th and 18th centuries, donated by Portland area residents. It sits on 46 acres of landscaped grounds that command a magnificent view of Portland from almost 1,000 feet above the city. *FYI: 3229 N.W. Pittock Drive, Portland, OR 97210; 503-823-3623.*

The **Flavel Mansion** (2) in Astoria is one of the finest examples of the Queen Anne Victorian architecture for which that city is know. Built by sea captain

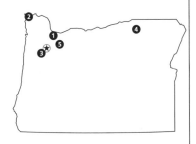

George Flavel, it is open to the public and contains displays of Victorian furnishings, art, and clothing. *FYI: 441 Eighth Street, Astoria; 503-325-2203.*

In Salem, adjacent to the Willamette University grounds, are two historic mansions, the **Bush House** (3) (*FYI: 600 Mission Street; 503-363-4714*) and the **Deepwood Estate** (*FYI: 1116 Mission Street; 503-363-1825*). Built in 1877, the Bush House preserves the furnishings and effects of a prominent Salem banker and publisher, while the Deepwood Estate displays collections of stained glass windows, period costumes, antique light fixtures, and apothecary bottles.

In eastern Oregon, visitors can see a different kind of historic home—the **Frazier Farmstead Museum** (4) near Pendleton. It is a vintage farmhouse with barns and antique agricultural equipment that shows what life in the region was like during the 1880s. Set among cherry, plum, and apple orchards, the farmhouse is surrounded with flower and herb gardens. *FYI: 541-938-4636.*

In the **Clackamas County Historical Society Museum** (5), Oregon City's history comes alive again. Oregon City's claims to fame include the Oregon Territory's first Protestant church (1840), first moonshine still (1842), first capital (1844), first jail (1844), first furniture factory (1844), first newspaper (1846), first Masonic lodge (1848), first coin mint (1849), and first fish ladder (1887), as well as America's first interurban electric railway (1893). *FYI: 503-655-5574.*

LOOKOUT CAMPING

Wilderness hikers and short-term hermits can rent one of Oregon's lookout stations that were used to watch for forest fires before radar and satellite technology made them obsolete. Originally designed to house rangers for weeks, the stations provide spartan lodging and the most spectacular mountain views in the state.
FYI: Gail Troop, USDA Forest Service, Pacific Northwest Region; 503-326-3644.

UNIQUE LODGING

● ●

Perhaps the finest bed and breakfast in Portland is aptly known as **Portland's White House** (1). Its stately architectural features include Greek columns and fountains. Each room has a different mood, such as the serene Garden Room, overlooking a fish pond and small waterfall, or the Balcony Room with its clawfoot tub and great view. *FYI: 1914 N.E. 22nd Avenue; 503-287-7131.*

Nine of the most popular state parks on the Oregon coast offer year-round camping in yurts—round, domed, Mongolian-style tents with wood floors, lights and electricity, and lockable doors. Campers who rent one of these yurts get bunk beds and an electric heater and bring their own bedding and other conveniences. *FYI: Oregon State Park Campsite Information Center; 800-452-5687.*

"Families Only" is the summertime rule at the **Rock Springs Guest Ranch** (2) near Bend. The ranch focuses on family-oriented programs that include fly-fishing, hayrides, horseback-riding, and mountain-biking. Kids get their own dining room—no parents allowed—and a special program of Earth Studies for Children. Stays are booked by the week and include all meals. In the off-season, the ranch gives up its family focus and serves as an executive conference center. *FYI: 541-382-1957.*

Crater Lake Lodge (3) , a rustic 80-room log lodge that dates back to the 1830s, has recently reopened after a five-year renovation. It is situated right on the rim of the volcano crater overlooking the lake. Rates are rela-

Oregon Caves National Monument

The chateau at Oregon Caves National Monument

tively inexpensive, but make reservations in advance. *FYI: Crater Lake Lodge Company; 541-594-2511.*

Another showplace historic lodge is **Timberline Lodge** (4), 6,000 feet up on the slope of Mount Hood. This 1937 landmark is noteworthy for the northwestern artwork on display as well as the craftsmanship of the decor and furnishings, products of a depression-era WPA program to support artists. Today it serves primarily as a ski lodge but is open—and popular—year-round. *FYI: 503-231-7979 or 800-452-1335.*

A creek flows right through the dining room of the **Oregon Caves Chateau** (5) at Oregon Caves National Monument. The lobby contains a massive double fireplace built from local marble. Built in 1934, the rustic six-story lodge hugs a hillside misty with waterfalls. *FYI: P.O. Box 128, Cave Junction, OR 97523; 541-592-3400.*

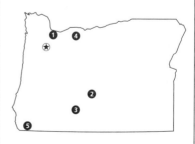

International Rose Test Gardens

The flower displays in the various gardens and parks peak in mid-June.

GREAT GARDENS

• •

Portland's **International Rose Test Gardens**, established in 1917, are the oldest continuously operating test gardens in the United States. The free gardens contain 10,000 plants and more than 400 varieties of roses, including hybrid roses named for Barbara Bush and Lucille Ball. As spectacular as the rose displays, however, is the view from the gardens' hillside location, overlooking downtown

Portland. On a clear day you can see Mount Hood and Mount St. Helens. *FYI: 400 S.W. Kingston Avenue, Portland, OR 97201; 503-823-3636.*

Nearby the International Rose Test Gardens, the 6-acre **Japanese Garden** is said to be the most authentic such garden outside Japan. Impeccably manicured trails lead to a teahouse, a pavilion, and five smaller gardens. *FYI: 611 S.W. Kingston Avenue, Portland, OR 97201; 503-223-4070.*

Another kind of Portland garden is found at **The Grotto** (National Sanctuary of Our Sorrowful Mother), a 62-acre sanctuary belonging to the Catholic Church. The flower garden surrounds a marble replica of Michelangelo's *Pietà* carved into the base of a cliff. An elevator carries visitors 110 feet up to the top of the cliff for a panoramic view of the Columbia River Valley and the Cascade Mountains. *FYI: N.E. 85th Avenue and Sandy Boulevard, Portland, OR 97220; 503-254-7371.*

The lavish formal gardens at **Shore Acres State Park** near Charleston were created by lumber baron Louis J. Simpson, who used profits from cutting the forests to create more than 100 acres of rose gardens, Japanese gardens, a lily pond, rhododendrons, and azaleas. His mansion burned to the ground more than 50 years ago, but his gardens have remained spectacular under the care of the state park service. *FYI: Cape Arago Highway; 541-888-3732.*

A footbridge at the Japanese Garden in Portland

Oregon Tourism Division

STATE
·················· of the ARTS

Ira Keller Memorial Fountain in downtown Portland

ART IN OREGON
· ·

E xpose Yourself to Art" was the slogan on a now-classic poster for the Portland Museum of Art which depicted an exhibitionist throwing his trenchcoat open in the direction a female marble sculpture. Although the flasher is only seen from behind, legend has it that the man was Oregon's eccentric governor, the late Tom McCall. Strange behavior, especially for a Republican.

Portland isn't the only city where art dealers host First Thursday Art Gallery Tours, but it may be the only one where transportation for the tours is by trolley. Colorfully painted replicas of Portland's original trolleys operate on the city's light rail line on the first Thursday evening of each month, shuttling people from the **Red Lion Hotel Lloyd Center** (*FYI: 1000 N.E. Multnomah; 503-323-7363*) to downtown gallery receptions. The free trolleys also run daily during the summer months and the Christmas shopping season, and on weekends year-round.

Although theater in Oregon is thought to revolve around the annual Shakespeare Festival in Ashland, the state also features a number of other theatrical opportunities. However, if you are hoping to catch some of the Ashland performances, be sure to plan ahead. Tickets sell out months in advance.

PORTLAND'S SCULPTURES AND FOUNTAINS

● ●

The 36-foot hammered copper statue, *Portlandia,* that stands at the Portland Building's entrance on Fifth Avenue between Main and Madison Streets in downtown Portland, is second in size only to the Statue of Liberty. When it was delivered in 1984, the statue, which is modeled after the image of "Lady Commerce" on the city seal, turned out to be too big to transport through the city streets, so it was floated up the Willamette River by barge and carried from Tom McCall Waterfront Park to its present location a few blocks away.

Beautifully sculpted in the form of four female figures, Portland's **Skidmore Fountain** (S.W. First Avenue at Ankeny Street) was designed to provide drinking water for horses, dogs, and people. Brass rings on the sides of the fountains used to hold public drinking cups.

Portland fountain art mimics nature in the **Ira Keller Memorial Fountain** (S.W. Fourth Avenue between Market and Clay Streets), where recirculating brooks tumble over a waterfall, and in the **Lovejoy Fountain** (Portland Center Building, S.W. Hall Street), where a concrete mountaintop spurts rivers that flow into a wading pool in a canyon below. The **Salmon Street Springs Fountain** has dozens of computer-controlled water jets that spray in changing patterns.

Oregon Tourism Division

Portlandia *keeps watch over her city*

For the 1888 grand opening of the Skidmore Fountain, local brewer Henry Weinhard offered to pump beer into the fountain if the city would provide the use of its fire hoses. City leaders vetoed the idea for fear that beer pirates would punch holes in the hoses.

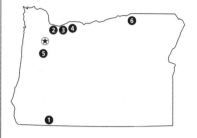

GETTING DRAMATIC

In Ashland, Shakespeare's plays are performed the way they were the first time, on the Elizabethan Stage, an exact reproduction of London's Fortune Theater (built in 1600).

1) Oregon Shakespeare Festival, the oldest in North America (started in 1935), runs from mid-February through October, though the outdoor Elizabethan Stage is only used in the summer. Audiences total more than 100,000 people each year. Besides the plays, the festival features concerts, lectures, a Shakespeare museum, and a backstage tour that takes visitors behind the scenes to see stagehands at work, dressing rooms, costumes, props, and the green room where actors relax when they're not on stage. *FYI: Box 158, Ashland, OR 97520; 541-482-4311.*

2) Portland Center Stage was formerly a branch of the Oregon Shakespeare Festival before it became independent in 1994. It broadened its range of presentations, offering five classic and contemporary plays each season. It's consistently cited as one of the best non-profit theaters in America. *FYI: 1111 S.W. Broadway, Portland, OR 97205; 503-248-6309.*

3) Tygres Heart Shakespeare Theatre performs Shakespeare in Portland in the fall and late spring, taking advantage of the Dolores Winningstad Theatre, an Elizabethan-style courtyard stage in the Portland Center for the Performing Arts. *FYI: 710 W. Madison, Suite 506, Portland, OR 97205; 503-222-9220.*

MORE OREGON THEATERS

• •

4) Portland Center for the Performing Arts is the largest stage complex in Oregon and fifth-largest in the U.S., entertaining more than one million people a year in four separate theaters. Its roster of resident companies includes the Portland Opera Association, Oregon Ballet Theatre, Oregon Children's Theater, Portland Community Concert Association, Oregon Symphony, Portland Arts and Lecture Series, Portland Youth Philharmonic, Institute for Science, Engineering and Public Policy, Portland Center Stage, The Musical Company, Tygres Heart Shakespeare Theatre, and Tear of Joy Puppet Theater. *FYI: 1111 Southwest Broadway, Portland; 503-248-4496.*

5) Eugene supports three theater groups: the **Actors Cabaret** and **Mainstage Theater** (*FYI: 530 W. 21st Street; 541-683-4368*), the **University Theater** (*FYI: University of Oregon campus; 541-687-5000*), and the **Very Little Theater** (*FYI: 2350 Hilyard Street; 541-344-7751*).

6) Happy Canyon Pageant, held outdoors in the evenings during the Pendleton Round-Up, re-creates the history of eastern Oregon. The show focuses on American Indians, settlers, and conflict between the two cultures. At the show's end, the whole audience is invited into the Happy Canyon Dance Hall, part of the stage set, for drinks, games of chance, and live country music. *FYI: P.O. Box 609, Pendleton, OR 97801; 800-457-6336.*

Happy Canyon Pageant participant

Matt Johnson

THEATERS ON THE SEA

The Playwrights American Conservatory Theater
FYI: 226 South Broadway; 541-269-2501 in Coos Bay.

The Newport Performing Arts Center
FYI: 777 West Olive Street; 541-265-9231 in Newport.

The Coaster Theater Playhouse
FYI: 108 North Hemlock Street; 503-436-1242 in Cannon Beach.

THE STINKERS

Not all movies shot in Oregon were classics. Here are some of the bombs.

- *The Apple Dumpling Gang* (1974) Bend
- *Rockaday Ritchie & Queen of the Hop* (1975) Portland
- *Meet the Raisins: The Story of the California Raisins* (1988) Portland
- *Teenage Mutant Ninja Turtles III* (1993) Astoria
- *The Great Elephant Chase* (1973) Rogue River

OREGON ON THE SILVER SCREEN

Since 1915, when the silent screen documentary *Where Cowboy is King* was shot in Pendleton, more than 230 feature films and made-for-TV movies have been filmed in Oregon. Some are classics, others most definitely aren't.

- *Peggy of the Secret Service* (1925) filmed in Portland
- *Call of the Wild* (1935) Mount Baker Lodge
- *Abe Lincoln in Illinois* (1939) Eugene, McKenzie River
- *Rachel and the Stranger* (1949) Eugene
- *Bend of the River* (1952) Mount Hood
- *The Day Called X* (1957) Portland
- *The Great Race* (1965) Gearhart
- *Paint Your Wagon* (1969) Baker
- *Five Easy Pieces* (1970) Eugene, Portland
- *Rooster Cogburn* (1974) Bend
- *One Flew Over the Cuckoo's Nest* (1975) Salem, Central Coast
- *National Lampoon's Animal House* 1977) Eugene, Cottage Grove
- *The Shining* (1977) Timberline Lodge
- *Black Stallion* (1978) Gearhart, Nehalem
- *Stand by Me* (1985) Eugene, Cottage Grove, Brownsville
- *Drugstore Cowboy* (1988) Portland
- *Kindergarten Cop* (1990) Astoria
- *My Own Private Idaho* (1990) Portland, Maupin
- *The River Wild* (1993) Grants Pass

Jack Oakie, Loretta Young, and Clark Gable in Call of the Wild

Archieve Photos

Visitors at the High Desert Museum south of Bend

ONE-OF-A-KIND MUSEUMS
••••••••••••••••••••••••••

The **American Advertising Museum** in Portland exhibits the world's largest collection of ads, from the first newspaper display advertisement in 1683 to television commercials. Also on display are classic Burma-Shave signs and a recording of the first radio commercial ever aired in the United States. *FYI: 9 N.W. 2nd Street; 503-226-0000.*

One of the best places to learn the more optimistic aspects of the timber industry both in Oregon and internationally is the **World Forestry Center** in Portland. The center displays a full range of exhibits on topics such as forest products and logging, old-growth forests, tropical rainforests, and forest fires. There is a show on the forests of the world, a gallery of wood carvings, and a 70-foot-tall "talking tree." Outside stands the 100-year-old Jessup Collection of 500 North American tree species. *FYI: 4033 S.W. Canyon Road, Portland, OR 97221; 503-228-1367.*

The **High Desert Museum** south of Bend defies classification. Part history museum, it contains Indian artifacts and documents from the Lewis and Clark expedition. It also has a gallery of fine western art as well as a zoological park, displaying living wild animals including owls, bats, porcupines, otters, and hawks. The museum's Center on the Spirit of the West re-creates the worlds of early Indians, explorers, and pioneers in an elaborate multimedia display. Outside, trails wind through 20 acres of desert land next

Oregon Tourism Division

to the museum, leading to an old sawmill and a settler's cabin. *FYI: 59800 South Hwy. 97, Bend, OR 97702; 541-382-4754.*

A fossil forest of petrified ancient trees blends into a living redwood forest outside the **Pacific Northwest Museum of Natural History**, illustrating the botanical changes that have taken place in southern Oregon over the past 20 million years. Inside, the big museum near the Southern Oregon State College Campus has exhibits that re-create Oregon's various ecosystems and lets visitors examine each natural environment through games, videos, microscopes, and computers. *FYI: 1500 E. Main Street, Ashland, OR 97520; 541-488-1084.*

The Pacific Northwest Museum of Natural History

Caroline Kopp

LITERARY OREGON

Author John Reed

L ebanese immigrant **Frederic Homer Balch** based *The Bridge of the Gods*, his popular 1890 fantasy novel of Indian life in primeval Oregon, on a local Indian legend about a natural rock bridge said to have arched across the Columbia River in ancient times.

Portland-born journalist **John Reed** is remembered for his 1919 book, *Ten Days that Shook the World*, an eyewitness account of the Russian Revolution. He moved to Moscow, where he was a celebrity. His tomb is in front of the Kremlin.

Oregon-born **Harold Lenoir Davis** was awarded the Pulitzer Prize in 1936 for his novel, *Honey in the Horn*. His other works include *Distant Music*, a memoir of life along the Columbia River.

Western writer **Ernest Haycox** wrote two dozen novels, but he is best remembered as a Hollywood screenwriter for cowboy movies of the 1930s and '40s, including *Stagecoach* and *Union Pacific*.

Bernard Malamud was a professor at Oregon State University in Corvallis from 1949 to 1961. During that time he wrote the novels *The Natural*, *The Assistant*, *A New Life*, and *The Magic Barrel*, which won a National Book Award. In 1966, he won a Pulitzer Prize for *The Fixer*.

Ontario, Oregon-born poet **Phyllis McGinley** was awarded the 1961 Pulitzer Prize for poetry for her collection, *Times Three: Selected Verse from Three Decades*. She is also remembered for her children's books such as *The Horse Who Lived Upstairs*.

Portland author **Ursula Le Guin** was

awarded both the Hugo and Nebula Awards for best science fiction novel of the year in 1969 for *The Left Hand of Darkness*. She won both awards again in 1972 for *The Dispossessed*.

Ken Kesey, a native of Springfield, Oregon, is best known for his novels *One Flew Over the Cuckoo's Nest* and *Sometimes a Great Notion*, both set in Oregon. His escapades in the 1960s hippie scene became the subject of Tom Wolfe's *The Electric Kool-Aid Acid Test*.

Short fiction master **Raymond Carver**, who was born and raised in Clatskanie, Oregon, won international acclaim for story collections such as *Cathedral* and *What We Talk About When We Talk About Love*. Transplanted to L.A., his stories inspired the 1993 film *Short Cuts*.

Author **Jean Auel** moved to Oregon with her family in 1957. In the primeval landscape of the Columbia Gorge she found the inspiration for her novels of prehistoric life, including *The Clan of the Cave Bears* and *The Valley of Horses*.

Poet Phyllis McGinley

Corbis-Bettmann

POWELL'S CITY OF BOOKS

• •

Powell's in Portland is the world's largest bookstore. With more than one million new and used books on its shelves, the main store covers an entire city block. Maps are given out to shoppers to guide them through the different categories. Powell's also operates a separate travel bookstore around the corner. *FYI: Main store—1005 West Burnside, Portland; 503-228-4651. Travel bookstore—701 Southwest Sixth Avenue, Portland; 503-228-1108.*

OREGON'S MUSIC SCENE

• •

Oregon's premier outdoor music venue is the **Britt Amphitheater**, an all-wood stage set among the pines on a hillside estate in Jacksonville, originally built by pioneer photographer Peter Britt. There are two consecutive Britt Festivals each summer. Concerts from mid-June through July showcase big-name performers in a full range of styles including jazz, rock, country-western, folk, modern dance, and musical comedy. In August, more than 90 professional musicians from all over the nation perform in the Britt Festival Orchestra for the Classical Festival, presenting eight completely different symphonic programs in three weeks. The festivals also include a series of prestigious workshops for student musicians and dancers. *FYI: Britt Festivals, P.O. Box 1124, Medford, OR 97501; 541-773-6077 or 800-882-7488.*

CONCERTS AT THE ZOO

• •

Those who love wild animals and music can indulge both passions at once on summer Wednesday and Thursday evenings, when Portland's **Metro Washington Park Zoo** presents public musical performances ranging from such long-standing traditions as "Your Zoo and All That Jazz" and "Zoograss" concerts to an innovative World Beat festival. The concerts are free with regular zoo admission. *FYI: 4001 S.W. Canyon Road, Portland, OR; 503-226-7627.*

D. Bjurstrom Studio/Oregon Tourism Division

JAZZ ON THE TRAIL
●●●●●●●●●●●●●●●●●●●●●●●●●

Britt Amphitheater in Jacksonville

A recent addition to the Oregon music scene, **The Trail Band** is a nine-member brass and string ensemble under the direction of jazz musician Cal Scott. The band travels around the state as part of the Portland Trail Blazers **Oregon Trail Celebration**, entertaining history buffs and music aficionados with its renditions of music that recalls the pioneer era. Performances include traditional folk music of the era along with original works by band member Marv Ross of Quarterflash. The group also performs at the opening of the Portland Trail Blazers pro basketball season.

Among the best-known musicians who come from Oregon are band leader Doc Severinsen, blues artist Curtis Salgado, and jazz greats Tom Grant and Michael Harrison.

THE SPORTING LIFE
....

SCENIC ROUTES AND DETOURS
● ●

1) Coast Highway is the most beautiful scenic drive in the United States. The road (U.S. 101) traces the entire 350 miles of Oregon's coastline from Brookings, near the California state line, to Astoria, where it crosses the bridge to Washington. Though traffic is often heavy, the drive takes motorists to all of the beaches, capes and headlands, lighthouses, and coastal villages that make up Oregon's most spectacular claim to fame. For the most enjoyable trip, allow two days.

2) Columbia Gorge Scenic Drive, a detour from Interstate 84 east of Portland, is 22 miles of natural splendor. The main attractions are a series of waterfalls, of which the highest is 620-foot Multnomah Falls. A nature trail leads into Oneonta Gorge—where the abundant plant life includes subspecies found nowhere else on earth—and a network of longer trails above the rim of the gorge in the Columbia Wilderness. The drive makes a good half-day trip from Portland and can be combined with a return drive by way of Mount Hood for an all-day loop trip.

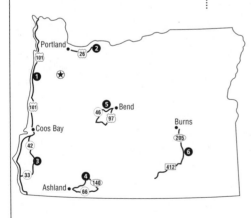

3) Inland River Route diverges from Highway 101 to follow the Coquille and Rogue Rivers through the southern Coast Range. Highlights include Coquille Myrtle Grove State Park and Hoffman Wayside Myrtlewood Grove, two of the finest stands of the beautiful hardwood tree unique to Oregon. This 120-mile route on paved back roads leaves the Coast Highway a few miles south of Coos Bay and rejoins it at Gold Beach. Allow a full day for a loop trip from either town, returning via the Coast Highway.

4) South Cascades Route follows the historic Applegate Trail (now Highway 66) west from Klamath Falls, then loops back on Highway 140 through the Klamath Basin, where Oregon's largest lake attracts up to one million birds in spring and fall, and through Rogue River National Forest to secluded Lake of the Woods before returning to Interstate 5 at Medford. It's 140 miles, so allow six hours.

5) Cascade Lakes Highway (Highway 46) leaves from Bend and climbs past Mount Bachelor into the heart of the high Cascades, providing access to a dozen beautiful mountain lakes and several trailheads for the Three Sisters Wilderness. The 75-mile route returns to main Highway 97 about 25 miles south of Bend. An all-day loop trip can include a stop at breathtaking Newberry National Volcanic Monument.

6) Lake Harney Scenic Byway (Highway 205 and County Road 412) takes motorists on a 200-mile expedition through southeastern Oregon's strange mix of desert, wetlands, and mountains from Burns to Lakeview through Malheur National Wildlife Refuge, Hart Mountain National Antelope Refuge, and the Warner Wetlands Area.

Steve Terrill/Oregon Tourism Division

Multnomah Falls can be seen from Columbia Gorge Scenic Drive

*Information on scenic drives is available from the **Oregon Economic Development Department, Tourism Division**, 775 Summer Street N.E., Salem, OR 97310; 503-986-0000.*

Biking in Willamette Valley

OREGON BY BIKE

O regon back roads and byways are ideal for bicycle touring, especially during the summer months. The state has widened scenic highways with special bicycle lanes.

The state's ultimate ride is the **Oregon Coast Bike Route**. It follows the Pacific shore for 367 miles, sometimes running alongside coastal Route 101 and other times veering off onto quiet back roads around capes and headlands well removed from highway traffic. The entire trip takes about one week. Bike rental places abound in coastal resort towns such as Cannon Beach and Seaside. On the Dry Side, another official bike route traces the old **Oregon Trail** from Hell's Canyon through John Day Country.

Newberry Volcanic National Monument is a good place to bike near Bend. Mountain bikes can be rented in town at High Cascade Descent. *FYI: 333 Riverfront Street; 541-389-0562.* Another magnificent spot for volcanic biking, suitable for either mountain bikes or touring tenspeeds, is the 33-mile paved Rim Drive around the lake in **Crater Lake National Park**.

When it comes to urban biking, **Eugene** has been rated by *Bicycling* magazine as one of the top ten cycling communities in the country because of its bicycle routes and facilities. The most beautiful ride in town is the bike path that runs along the Willamette River from Cogburn Road south to Copping Street. Rental bikes are available at Pedal Power. *FYI: 545 High Street; 541-687-1775.*

One of the most pleasant spots for biking in the Portland area is the wildlife sanctuary at **Sauvie Island**. Bicycles are for rent in Portland at **Glacier's Edge** (*FYI: 8775 Southwest Canyon Lane; 503-297-4747*) and Agape Cycle (*FYI: 2610 Southeast Clinton Street; 503-230-0317*).

Cyclists who prefer to travel in a group with a guide, a "sag wagon," and logistical support should check out **Pathfinders**, a bicycle touring company located in a rural area east of Eugene. It offers bike rides to mountain lakes high in the Cascades. *FYI: 541-782-4838.* In Bend, **Wanderlust Tours** organizes bike expeditions to Lava Lands, the Cascade Lakes Road, and even Crater Lake. *FYI: 800-661-5878.*

The Oregon Department of Transportation can send you a free bike touring map. FYI: Room 200, Transportation Building, Salem, OR 97310; 503-378-3432.

Pathfinders offers low-traffic bike tours throughout the Cascades

INTO THE
WILDERNESS

● ●

Oregon has no less than 35 federally designated wilderness areas—large roadless expanses of public land that are protected from most commercial exploitation. Wheeled vehicles, including mountain bikes—are prohibited in these wilderness areas. Visitors can explore them only on foot, horseback, cross-country skis or snowshoes, or by boat. Almost all of them are in the higher altitudes of Oregon's 13 national forests. Steep mountain slopes prevented road-building and logging in earlier times, before the government began protecting wilderness areas.

The largest wilderness area in Oregon is the **Eagle Cap Wilderness** in the Wallowa Mountains in the northeast corner of the state. It contains more than half of Oregon's mountain peaks over 9,000 feet high. Hundreds of miles of trails link eight valleys that radiate in all directions from glacier-capped summits in the heart of the wilderness. For those who lack the time or inclination to trek into the wilderness, its full splendor can be seen from the summit of 8,256-foot Mount Howard, which can be reached from the Wallowa Lake Tramway (*FYI: 541-432-5331*) near the town of Joseph.

The **Pacific Crest Trail**, the longest hiking trail in the United States, runs from the Canadian border to the Mexican border. It crosses the Columbia River to enter Oregon at Cascade Locks and continues for some 350 miles along the highest reaches of the Cascade Range to cross the California state line south of Ashland. The Oregon segment of the trail strings nine wilderness areas, a national park, and an Indian reservation together like a pearl necklace. Although parts of the trail require specialized equipment and technical mountaineering skills, other areas such as Crater Lake National Park and the Mount Washington Wilderness north of McKenzie Pass are popular routes for day or weekend hikes.

LLAMAS MAKE TREKKING EASY

● ●

The east side of the Cascades is one of North America's top llama breeding areas. Since the 1970s, breeders in this part of Oregon have been renting llamas to wilderness hikers to carry their camping gear or even young children on weekend excursions into the roadless high country. The area around Sisters, a small mountain town high on the dry side of the Cascades, within a short drive of three major wilderness areas, is home to more than 6,000 llamas—and 765 human inhabitants. *FYI: Oregon Llamas, Box 6, Camp Sherman, OR; 541-595-2088.*

The vast wilderness areas of the Wallowa Mountains in northeastern Oregon are becoming another popular llama-trekking area. *FYI: Hurricane Creek Llama Treks, 63366 Pine Tree Road, Enterprise, OR; 541-432-4455.*

Since 1985, some llama breeders have also started raising their shorter, rounder relatives, alpacas. Though less useful than llamas as hiking companions, the alpacas produce some of the world's most valuable wool—nine times warmer than sheep's wool.

Llamas in central Oregon

Gene Johnson/Oregon Tourism Division

*Llamas from the Andes were bred by the Incas centuries ago to carry loads of supplies up mountain trails. You can pet a llama at **Northwest Alpacas**, 11785 S.W. River Road, Hillsboro, OR; 503-257-2227.*

Participants at Albany Timber Carnival

SPECTATOR SPORTS

• •

The largest rodeo in the Pacific Northwest is the **Pendleton Round-Up**. Held every year since 1910, the four-day extravaganza is reputed to be the fastest-moving rodeo on the circuit. Besides the seven standard Professional Rodeo Cowboys Association-sanctioned events (bareback bronc riding, saddle bronc riding, bull riding, steer wrestling, calf roping, steer roping, and team roping), the Round-Up features such unlikely contests as pony express races, wild horse races, and wild cow milking.

The **Albany Timber Carnival** is to environmental activists what rodeos are to animal rights activists—a bunch of grown men and women playing traditional but politically incorrect games. Nevertheless, thousands of spectators come to Albany on Fourth of July Weekend to see lumber-jacks from around the world compete with local Oregonians for more than $25,000 in cash prizes in the world's largest logging event. Contests include bucking (sawing), tree topping, log chopping, speed climbing, birling (log rolling in water), and axe throwing.

PORTLAND'S PROFESSIONAL TEAMS

Portland has no pro football or baseball team, but it does have several other professional sports teams:

The **Portland Trail Blazers** (called simply "the Blazers") basketball team made the NBA Playoffs for 12 consecutive years and holds the record for the most consecutive sold-out home games of any NBA team—769. The sell-out streak lasted until the Blazers moved to their new home, the 20,000-seat Rose Garden Arena, twice the size of their former home, Memorial Coliseum.

The **Portland Winter Hawks** are one of the most successful teams in the Western Hockey League, with six division titles and the 1983 Memorial Cup to their credit. Many Winter Hawks players have gone on to play in the National Hockey League, including NHL All-Star Cam Neely.

Portland has virtually year-round hockey. During the summer months, when there are no Winter Hawks hockey games, fans support the **Portland Rage** roller hockey team. More than a spectator sport, the Rage invites fans to skate alongside the pros during pre-game warm-ups.

HIGH-SPEED SPORTS

Portland Meadows
FYI: 1001 North Schmeer Road, Portland, OR 97217; 503-285-9144

Multnomah Greyhound Park
FYI: 223rd and N.E. Glisan, Portland, OR 97024; 503-667-7700.

Portland International Raceway
One of 16 Indy Car racing tracks in the world. Also hosts other races including go-carts, motocross, bicycle, and roller-blade races.
FYI: 1940 North Victory Boulevard, Portland, OR 97217; 503-285-6635

Portland Malibu Grand Prix
Amateur race car drivers can experience racing thrills firsthand.
FYI: 9405 Southwest Cascade Avenue, Beaverton, OR 97005; 503-641-8122.

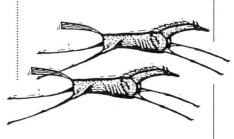

OREGON ROCKS

• •

Climbing Monkey Face at Smith Rock State Park

In the lonely, mostly unpopulated reaches of eastern Oregon, most of the landmarks are rocks. Here are some of the region's most unusual geological oddities, favorites of rock climbers and rockhounds alike:

Smith Rock ranks as Oregon's most popular site for technical rock climbing. Located on the Crooked River west of Prineville, the rock is actually a cluster of vertical stone columns 300 to 500 feet in height, with climbing areas suitable for every skill level. There is even one monolith—named Monkey Face—that is considered impossible to scale, though that fact does not deter climbers from attempting it.

To the east of Prineville stands **Stein's Pillar**, a solitary stone column that rises 350 feet out of the pine forest. The pillar was originally a small volcano that eroded away to leave only its hard lava core, so unusual in appearance that sightseers drive for nine miles down unpaved forest service roads and hike for another mile to snap photos of it.

The **Albert Rim**, the longest exposed earthquake fault in North America, rises from the sun-crackled Alvord Desert to form a wall several hundred feet thick separating the tiny southern Oregon town of Burns from Malheur Lake. The rock wall extends for 25 miles.

The crater that is now **Fort Rock State Park** in southern Oregon was once a tall, active volcano. As the climate changed, a large lake gradually formed around the volcano's base, transforming it into an island. Water erosion nibbled away at the slopes that separated the lake from the red-hot center of the volcano crater—until the volcano sprung a leak. When the water poured in, it turned to superheated steam, which caused an explosion that completely destroyed the mountain, leaving only a 325-foot-tall rim of lava from the center of the crater.

American Indians crossed the sagebrush desert of southeastern Oregon to mine material for arrow and spear points, knives, and scrapers from **Glass Buttes**, one of the world's largest obsidian deposits. While this volcanic molten glass is common in Oregon, only here was obsidian found in colors besides black. The Indians prized it so highly that points from Glass Buttes were traded as far away as the Ohio River—a longer distance than that covered by Lewis and Clark.

ROCKHOUNDS' DELIGHT

A mong rock collectors from neighboring California and Washington, Oregon has a near-legendary reputation as a happy hunting ground for semiprecious and just plain strange mineral specimens. Agates polished by the sea are found in profusion on **Agate Beach** near Newport. Huge deposits of obsidian are found near Newberry Crater and at Glass Buttes. But the most sought-after trophies, "thunder eggs," are found in several areas around Prineville. These round, hollow agates, often four to six inches in diameter, formed inside bubbles in lava flows from ancient volcanoes. The thrill comes not only in finding a thunder egg but in sawing it in half to discover the beautiful crystals some of them contain.

Newberry Crater

Rick Schafer/Oregon Tourism Division

SPIRIT of OREGON

····················

Bridge of the Gods

STRANGE TALES

· ·

THE BRIDGE OF THE GODS

The present-day Bridge of the Gods, which arcs across the Columbia River at Cascade Locks, takes its name from an old Indian legend. The original bridge is said to have been a natural stone span across the Columbia Gorge above The Dalles. (It would have been by far the largest natural bridge on earth.) According to the story, two Indian gods who were brothers ruled opposite banks of the river, and both of them fell in love with the same woman. The rivals fought a duel, throwing flaming rocks at each other across the river, but the rocks rained down on the Bridge of the Gods, causing it to crack and fall into the river. The young men's father grew so angry that he turned everybody involved to stone. The brothers became Mount Hood and Mount Adams, and their beloved became Mount St. Helens. The wreckage of the bridge became Celilo Falls, where Indians used to catch salmon with nets. Don't look for the falls today, though. Like the original Bridge of the Gods, they have vanished forever into legend, flooded by the completion of The Dalles Dam in 1957.

The Dalles Dam

Rod Furgason/Unicorn Stock Photos

THE BLUE BUCKET

According to a persistent old tale, an early pioneer wagon train bound for the Willamette Valley stopped to rest by a creek somewhere along the trail that is now U.S. Highway 20 east of Burns. While there, the children collected a blue bucket full of shiny yellow pebbles. The menfolk discovered that the pebbles were made of metal soft enough to be hammered into fishing sinkers. When they moved on, they left the gleaming pebbles behind. In those days, gold had not yet been discovered anywhere in the United States, so it never occurred to the pioneers that the pebbles might be valuable. Later, during the California Gold Rush, the bucket-of-gold story spread far and wide. Although several small gold strikes were made in the region while searching for "the Blue Bucket," the creek full of gold nuggets has never been found.

Ryan Bond

A wedding at the Church of Elvis

OREGON ODDITIES

Portland's strangest tourist attraction, the **Church of Elvis** is a 24-hour streetfront spiritual smorgasbord. The multimedia window display in front of this outrageously kitschy gift shop features a computer on which the King himself (Elvis, that is) transmits cosmic e-mail answers to all your questions about life, death, God, and rock-and-roll. A few more quarters will get you a reading by the world's cheapest psychic, or a sermon that includes a photo opportunity with the King. ***FYI:*** *720 S.W. Ankeny, Portland, OR 97205; 503-226-3671.*

PORTLAND'S LEPRECHAUN HABITAT

Mill Ends Park, the world's smallest city park, is located in a median strip at the corner of Front Avenue and Taylor Street. The 24-inch-square park got its start in the 1970s when Dick Fagan, a columnist for *The Oregonian*, planted flowers in a pothole outside his office window and gave the tiny "park" its name. As he reported on the adventures of Patrick O'Toole, a leprechaun who lived there, Fagan's creation became such a part of Portland lore that the city parks department finally made its park designation official.

Portland also boasts the largest city park in the United States—5,000-acre **Forest Park**. There have been no leprechaun sightings in this park, though.

BEAVER MONEY

During the 1849 gold rush in neighboring California, the Oregon Exchange Company minted "Beaver Money"—$5 and $10 gold coins stamped with the image of Oregon's favorite rodent. Putting this alternative money in circulation allowed the economy of the new territory to grow faster than it otherwise could have with the limited amount of U.S. currency that reached the Pacific Northwest.

THE GURU OF ANTELOPE

The tiny ranching community of Antelope (pop. 35) gained national notoriety in the early 1980s when Bhagwan Sri Rajneesh moved there. The guru originally picked the location, about as far as one can live from modern mainstream civilization, for the quiet, peace, and spiritual freedom he hoped to find there for himself and his followers.

Soon, however, his 100-square-mile ranch, dubbed Rajneeshpuram, was inhabited by thousands of "Rajneeshees," and sightseers who came to see the sect's commune—which eventually developed gift shops, restaurants, and even a disco—numbered more than 100,000 in a single year.

The final indignity came when sect members outvoted the locals and changed the town's name to Rajneesh. Old-time Antelope citizens begged their congressman for help, and soon IRS agents found the guru liable for millions in back taxes. Rajneesh was deported, his followers scattered, and ranchers voted unanimously to restore the name.

*Portland is the only city in the United States that has a volcano—**Mount Tabor**—within its municipal limits.*

Corbis-Bettmann

Bhagwan Sri Rajneesh

Governor Tom McCall

Tom McCall became known for his bumper stickers urging tourists to visit Washington, Idaho, Montana—any place but Oregon. The idea was to keep the state from being discovered by Californians.

POLITICS

• •

Known as the torchbearer of Oregon's tradition of "Republican radicalism," the late **Tom McCall** served as governor in the late 1960s and early 1970s. McCall gained national prominence for his environmental stances, drawing on the ideas of Ralph Nader, Eugene McCarthy, John Gardner, Cesar Chavez, and American Indian leaders. The unconventional politician was once quoted by *The Oregonian* as saying, "I probably wouldn't be a Republican in any state but this one."

DO-IT-YOURSELF LAWMAKING

• •

In an effort to clean up the corruption that had tainted Oregon politics through the last years of the nineteenth century, Portland activist **William U'Ren** led a campaign for initiative and referendum laws. Unique when they were passed in 1902 and only used in a few other states today, these laws let citizens put proposed laws on the ballot by gathering petition signatures and then decide by popular vote whether they will be enacted.

Initiative and referendum have been used to achieve a number of progressive goals—among them, women's suffrage, a school voucher system, a statewide health care plan, and the country's first bottle bill. The procedure has also been used for less admirable aims, such as attempts to strip African Americans of voting rights, to abolish Catholic schools, and to prevent the passage of laws protecting gay and lesbian Oregonians from discrimination.

WOMEN'S RIGHTS AND OREGON POLITICS

• •

Women won the right to vote in Oregon in 1912, largely through the efforts of suffragist **Abigail Scott Duniway**. She was a columnist for a weekly Portland newspaper and urged the use of Oregon's initiative and referendum laws to put women's rights on the ballot. Voting rights for women were defeated for three consecutive years, but in the end, Oregon became one of the earliest states to recognize women's suffrage rights.

ETHNIC PORTLAND

• •

Visitors enter Portland's Chinatown through a magnificent ceremonial gate located at N.W. Fourth Avenue and Burnside Street. The gate was a gift from Portland's Chinese sister city, Kaohsiung. Beyond it lies a district of bright red facades, cherry trees, and Oriental lamp poles that has traditionally been the city's Chinese American neighborhood since the 19th century.

Portland's citizens of Japanese descent are honored at the **Japanese-American Historical Plaza**, a sculpture garden shaded by cherry trees at the north end of **Tom McCall Waterfront Park**. The plaza is dedicated to the thousands of Japanese Americans who were relocated from Portland to detention camps during World War II. Several of the largest camps were located in eastern Oregon, and families of the people who were interned there account for much of Portland's large Japanese American community.

Portland has a sister-city relationship with Guadalajara, Mexico. Although Portland's Hispanic population is relatively small, the city's annual Cinco de Mayo Festival at Tom McCall Waterfront Park is one of its biggest annual events.

Rose Parade

OREGON FESTIVALS

The biggest all-floral parade in the United States is just one of the highlights of the annual **Portland Rose Festival**, which features more than eighty community events ranging from rose shows to rodeos and from art gallery tours to mountain bike races. Among the most unusual contests in the six-week summer extravaganza are Chinese dragon boat races, a lawn bowling tournament, and a race in boats made from milk cartons.

Exhibitions include woodcarving, egg artistry, and, of course, rose art in all media. The festival climaxes with the Rose Festival Airshow, one of the nation's top airshows. More than two million people flock to Portland each year for the festival. *FYI: Held from the beginning of June through mid-July.*

Eugene's **Oregon Country Fair** has its roots in the early-1970s Oregon Renaissance Faire. Charging trademark infringement, the promoters of an older Renaissance festival in California succeeded in obtaining a court order to shut down the fair in Eugene. But the event refused to go away. Instead, organizers simply changed the name, and little by little the Country Fair has changed character to re-create a more recent, equally colorful historical era—the Sixties hippie scene. Thousands of genuine old-fashioned hippies who live in isolated Oregon backcountry communities gather at the Oregon Country Fair, exuberantly sharing the festivities with a younger generation of free souls from every corner of Oregon, with live entertainment and hundreds of arts-and-crafts vendors. *FYI: Held in late July.*

CALENDAR

• •

Here's a short calendar of other one-of-a-kind festivals you might or might not want to miss:

APRIL: Eugene holds its annual **Jello Art Show**, and Hood River hosts the **Oregon Open Bench Press Tournament.**

MAY: Wool is the focus of Salem's **Sheep to Shawl Festival**, and Coburg sponsors its **Colossal Clutter Cleanout.** The most obscure ethnic festival of the month is Bend's **Amerikanvak—Basques in the High Desert** celebration.

JUNE: Corvallis hosts the **Beatlefest Concert** and Winston holds **Oregon's Original City-Wide Garage Sale.**

JULY: Vale invites visitors from across the state to its annual **Rodeo and Suicide Race**, while Nyssa celebrates its rocks during **Thunderegg Days**. Monument holds a **Grasshopper Roping Festival.**

AUGUST: Milton-Freewater holds its renowned **Muddy Frogwater Festival**, Monmouth its **Victorian Tea Festival**, and Hood River its **Train Robbery Celebration**, all annual events.

SEPTEMBER: The big athletic event at The Dalles is the **Aluminum Man Triathlon.** Grants Pass hosts their popular **Antique Car Parts Show.**

OCTOBER: Don't miss the **Reptile and Amphibian Show** in Portland. Reedsport hosts **Spider Night.**

If you want to enter the ***Silver Trails Slug Race*** *at the Rhododendron Festival in Florence, you can rent one of the slimy little critters from a local entrepreneur for a small fee.* ***FYI:*** *Held the third weekend in May.*

WEATHERING THE WEATHER

In a western Oregon winter, the sun may never shine at all for a period of three to four months. This can give rise to a chronic low-level depression which doctors refer to as Seasonal Affective Disorder (S.A.D.), but which is known (all too well) to locals as the "Oregon blues." Here's a grab bag of hints from Oregon old-timers on how to cope with the clammy climate:

1) Wear a hat and squishy tennis shoes and go hiking in the rain, golfing in the rain, rollerblading in the rain, driving your convertible with the top down in the rain, or beachcombing and perhaps working on your raintan. Rubber boots, deemed an Eastern affectation, are not sold in Oregon, and umbrellas are reserved for emergency use in serious storms.

2) Install lots of high-wattage floodlights and infrared heat lamps in every room of the house. If you still feel depressed, put travel posters of Hawaii on all the walls.

3) Fly to Hawaii and stay there until spring.

4) If your boss won't let you migrate to Hawaii for the winter, drive over to the eastern side of the Cascades and spend the whole weekend in a Dry Side town such as Pendleton. The thermometer may plunge to -28°

An Oregonian poll several years ago revealed that two-thirds of Portlanders actually enjoy rain.

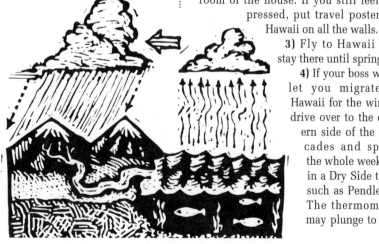

Oregon Tourism Division

Washington County

or so, but at least the sun shines practically every day.

5) If you're feeling a little blue in Portland, remind yourself that the 37.6" annual precipitation is actually less than that of Atlanta, Baltimore, or Houston. If that doesn't work, remind yourself it is less than half the rainfall of nearby Astoria, which averages 77.4" annually.

6) If you live in Astoria, remind yourself how lucky you are to live where it rarely snows. Sort of like Tucson, only grayer, isn't it? If you can't get yourself to buy that line, see hint number 3.

7) Resist the temptation to take a comprehensive tasting tour of Oregon's 28 microbreweries and 112 independent wineries in your own living room.

8) Both Portland and Eugene have more and bigger bookstores per capita than almost any other city in North America.

KIDS'
········ ADVENTURES

Oregon Tourism Division

Taking pictures at Metro Washington Park Zoo

ZOOS, AQUARIUMS, AND SUCH
•••••••••••••••••••••••••

Portland's **Metro Washington Park Zoo** replicates animal habitats from all over the globe. The newest exhibit area—a rainforest exhibit that seems to fit right in with the soggy Portland climate—houses pythons, crocodiles, and bats from the Congo. Nearby, antelopes and zebras roam the African veldt. There's even an Arctic exhibit with musk oxen and grizzly bears, and another where penguins cavort around a reproduction of the rocky cliffs of Tierra del Fuego, the tip of South America. This zoo boasts the world's largest captive breeding program for Asian elephants, and most people will never have another chance to see as many elephants at one time. The zoo also has the largest chimpanzee population in the United States. *FYI: 4001 S.W. Canyon Road, Portland, OR; 503-226-7627.*

Also in Portland, the **Oregon Museum of Science and Industry** (OMSI) is considered one of the finest centers of its kind in the United States. The museum features dozens of hands-on exhibits for kids, including computer games, science labs, and tornado and earthquake simulations. Through OMSI's glass walls, visitors can enjoy prime views of nearby Willamette River.

WILDLIFE SAFARI

Wildlife Safari near Roseburg features animals from Africa and other exotic places in a 600-acre drive-through park. You have to keep the windows rolled up because of the lions and bears, but there's a separate petting zoo and an elephant kids can ride. *FYI: 541-679-6761.*

The state's largest aquarium, the **Oregon Coast Aquarium** in Newport gives you a chance to see 200 species of sea creatures close-up. The artificial habitat built along four acres of Yaquina Bay contains replicas of tide pools, cliffs, and sea caves, where you can view seals, sea lions, sea otters and a giant octopus through underwater windows. There are indoor tanks for fish, jellyfish, mollusks, crabs, sea anemones, and many other species. There is even a touch tank where you can see what a starfish feels like. The aquarium also has the largest walk-through seabird aviary in North America. *FYI: S.E. Ferry Slip Road, Newport, OR 97365; 541-867-3474.*

Everything is extinct at **Prehistoric Gardens**, located on Highway 101 between Port Orford and Gold Beach. Set amid one of the finest remaining stands of coastal rain forest, the life-sized dinosaurs in this park are labors of love that have made this their home since 1955, when certified public accountant Ernest V. Nelson created this showplace for his unusual hobby. The largest of the dinosaurs, a brachiosaurus, is 86 feet long and 46 feet tall. *FYI: 541-332-4463.*

WESTERN DEER PARK AND ARBORETUM

This park and arboretum near Sheridan has deer and other animal species native to Oregon, as well as 120 different species of trees for them to hide behind. *FYI: Highway 18; 503-843-2152.*

Castle at Enchanted Forest

Oaks Park Amusement Park in Portland features one of the biggest pipe organs in the United States.

AMUSEMENT PARKS

● ●

Portland's **Oaks Park Amusement Park,** surrounded by forest just a few minutes from downtown, offers year-round fun including roller skating on the largest skating rink in the Pacific Northwest, as well as international food booths, a full range of amusement park rides, and a children's theater. ***FYI:*** *Located at Sellwood Bridge; 503-236-9143.*

Enchanted Forest in the town of Turner, south of Salem, features Fort Fearless, the Tofteville Mining Town, and an Old World Village, as well as a haunted house and a bobsled run. There's also a medieval castle, the Seven Dwarfs' Mine, and an outdoor children's theater. *FYI: 8462 Enchanted Way S.E.; 503-371-4242.*

Just down the road is **Thrillville U.S.A.**, home of the largest roller coaster in Oregon as well as two open-tube waterslides, bumper cars and boats, miniature golf, and an octopus ride. The newest thrill, the Skycoaster, accelerates a hang-gliding apparatus and its passengers from 0 to 60 mph in 1.79 seconds—90 feet above the ground. *FYI: 8372 Enchanted Way S.E.; 503-363-4095.*

PLANET EARTH CALLING

You can send a message into space using a hands-on computer at the **Oregon Museum of Science and Industry**, the fifth-largest science museum in the United States. The museum also has laser light shows, a room where you can experience a simulated earthquake measuring 5.5 on the Richter Scale, and the USS Blueback submarine, used in filming *The Hunt for Red October. FYI: 1945 S.E. Water Avenue, Portland; 503-797-4000.*

ART MEETS NATURE

The **Sitka Center for Art and Ecology**, located near Cascade Head, offers summer workshops where kids of all ages can not only learn to identify plants and birds under the tutelage of resident ecologists, but also practice a full range of arts such as Siletz Indian basketry, wood block printing, and quilt making. *FYI: Neskowin Coast Foundation, P.O. Box 65, Otis, OR 97368.*

INDEX

INDEX

Other Books from John Muir Publications

Rick Steves' Books

Asia Through the Back Door, 400 pp., $17.95

Europe 101: History and Art for the Traveler, 352 pp., $17.95

Mona Winks: Self-Guided Tours of Europe's Top Museums, 432 pp., $18.95

Rick Steves' Baltics & Russia, 144 pp., $9.95

Rick Steves' Europe, 528 pp., $17.95

Rick Steves' France, Belgium & the Netherlands, 256 pp., $13.95

Rick Steves' Germany, Austria & Switzerland, 256 pp., $13.95

Rick Steves' Great Britain, 240 pp., $13.95

Rick Steves' Italy, 224 pp., $13.95

Rick Steves' Scandinavia, 192 pp., $13.95

Rick Steves' Spain & Portugal, 208 pp., $13.95

Rick Steves' Europe Through the Back Door, 480 pp., $18.95

Rick Steves' French Phrase Book, 176 pp., $5.95

Rick Steves' German Phrase Book, 176 pp., $5.95

Rick Steves' Italian Phrase Book, 176 pp., $5.95

Rick Steves' Spanish & Portuguese Phrase Book, 304 pp., $6.95

Rick Steves' French/ German/Italian Phrase Book, 320 pp., $7.95

A Natural Destination Series

Belize: A Natural Destination, 344 pp., $16.95

Costa Rica: A Natural Destination, 380 pp., $18.95

Guatemala: A Natural Destination, 360 pp., $16.95

For Birding Enthusiasts

The Birder's Guide to Bed and Breakfasts: U.S. and Canada, 416 pp., $17.95

The Visitor's Guide to the Birds of the Central National Parks: U.S. and Canada, 400 pp., $15.95

The Visitor's Guide to the Birds of the Eastern National Parks: U.S. and Canada, 400 pp., $15.95

The Visitor's Guide to the Birds of the Rocky Mountain National Parks: U.S. and Canada, 432 pp., $15.95

Unique Travel Series

All are 112 pages and $10.95 paperback, except Georgia and Oregon.

Unique Arizona
Unique California
Unique Colorado
Unique Florida
Unique Georgia ($11.95)
Unique New England
Unique New Mexico
Unique Oregon ($9.95)
Unique Texas
Unique Washington

Travel+Smart™ Trip Planners

All are 256 pages and $14.95 paperback.

American Southwest Travel+Smart™ Trip Planner

Colorado Travel+Smart™ Trip Planner (avail. 9/96)

Eastern Canada Travel+Smart™ Trip Planner

Hawaii Travel+Smart™ Trip Planner

Kentucky/Tennessee Travel+Smart™ Trip Planner (avail. 9/96)

Minnesota/Wisconsin
Travel+Smart™ Trip Planner
(avail. 10/96)
New England Travel+Smart™ Trip
Planner
Pacific Northwest Travel+Smart™
Trip Planner (avail. 8/96)

Other Terrific Travel Titles

The 100 Best Small Art Towns in
America, 256 pp., $15.95
The Big Book of Adventure
Travel, 384 pp., $17.95
Indian America: A Traveler's
Companion, 480 pp., $18.95
The People's Guide to Mexico,
608 pp., $19.95
Ranch Vacations: The Complete
Guide to Guest and Resort,
Fly-Fishing, and Cross-Country
Skiing Ranches, 528 pp., $19.95
Understanding Europeans,
272 pp., $14.95
Undiscovered Islands of the
Caribbean, 336 pp., $16.95
Watch It Made in the U.S.A.:
A Visitor's Guide to the
Companies that Make Your
Favorite Products, 328 pp.,
$16.95
The World Awaits, 280 pp., $16.95

Automotive Titles

The Greaseless Guide to Car
Care, 272 pp., $19.95
How to Keep Your Subaru Alive,
480 pp., $21.95
How to Keep Your Toyota Pickup
Alive, 392 pp., $21.95
How to Keep Your VW Alive,
464 pp., $25

Ordering Information

Please check your local bookstore
for our books, or call **1-800-888-
7504** to order direct and to receive
a complete catalog. A shipping
charge will be added to your
order total.

Send all inquiries to:
John Muir Publications
P.O. Box 613
Santa Fe, NM 87504